Centered on Success

Centered on Success
Grade One

Reinforce essential skills while promoting independent learning with the kid-pleasing center activities in *Centered on Success* for grade one! We've designed 20 all-new center activities to help you reinforce language arts and math skills through appropriately challenging learning experiences. Each center is adapted to two different skill levels or tasks, so you can match each activity to individual students' needs. For convenience, the two levels are color coded—yellow and blue—for easy identification and management. Simply choose a specific level for each student to complete, or encourage each child through both levels (first yellow, then blue). If appropriate, have each child complete the accompanying reinforcing skill sheet after he has successfully completed a blue level center.

Each center contains all the basic materials you need, including full-color, tear-out pages for easy center setup and implementation. Also included for your convenience are full-color center labels, a center management checklist, and motivating student awards.

Each center includes the following:
- an easy-to-scan teaching page with a skill description for each instructional level, a list of provided materials, step-by-step directions for preparing and using the center, and one or more center options for enhancing or extending the activity
- a full-color center mat, suitable for laminating
- first-level activity cards (yellow) programmed for self-checking
- second-level activity cards (blue) programmed for self-checking
- a recording sheet or a reproducible skill sheet suitable for additional reinforcement and assessment of a featured skill

Setting up the centers:
1. Tear out the perforated pages: teaching page, recording sheet, or skill sheet (on back of teaching page), center mat, leveled activity cards.
2. Make a master copy of the student skill sheet.
3. Cut apart each set of leveled activity cards (yellow and blue).
4. Laminate the center mat and activity cards for durability.
5. Store the cards in resealable plastic bags. Place all center pieces in a large string-tie envelope. Label and store as desired.
6. Laminate the yellow and blue center signs on pages 5 and 7.

Managing the centers:
1. Make a copy of the center checklist on page 6. Program the sheet with students' names and the center titles.
2. Choose a center and decide which level each student will complete.
3. Using a yellow or blue highlighter, mark the appropriate cell on the center checklist to indicate the level each student will complete. Set the checklist aside.
4. Place the center materials at a single-student center area. Post the appropriate yellow or blue label.
5. Upon each student's completion of the center, assess understanding and mark the center checklist for each child accordingly.

Managing Editor: Allison E. Ward
Editor at Large: Diane Badden
Staff Editors: Kimberly A. Brugger, Cindy Daoust
Concept Developers: Virginia Conrad, Bonnie Mertzlufft
Copy Editors: Tazmen Carlisle, Amy Kirtley-Hill, Kristy Parton, Debbie Shoffner, Cathy Edwards Simrell
Art Coordinator: Rebecca Saunders
Artists: Jennifer Tipton Bennett, Pam Crane, Chris Curry, Theresa Lewis Goode, Clevell Harris, Ivy L. Koonce, Clint Moore, Greg D. Rieves, Rebecca Saunders, Barry Slate, Donna K. Teal
The Mailbox® Books.com: Judy P. Wyndham (MANAGER); Jennifer Tipton Bennett (DESIGNER/ARTIST); Karen White (INTERNET COORDINATOR); Paul Fleetwood, Xiaoyun Wu (SYSTEMS)

President, The Mailbox Book Company™: Joseph C. Bucci
Director of Book Planning and Development: Chris Poindexter
Curriculum Director: Karen P. Shelton
Book Development Managers: Cayce Guiliano, Elizabeth H. Lindsay, Thad McLaurin
Editorial Planning: Kimberley Bruck (DIRECTOR); Debra Liverman, Sharon Murphy, Susan Walker (TEAM LEADERS)
Editorial and Freelance Management: Karen A. Brudnak; Sarah Hamblet, Hope Rodgers (EDITORIAL ASSISTANTS)
Editorial Production: Lisa K. Pitts (TRAFFIC MANAGER); Lynette Dickerson (TYPE SYSTEMS); Mark Rainey (TYPESETTER)
Librarian: Dorothy C. McKinney

Manufactured in the United States
10 9 8 7 6 5 4 3 2 1

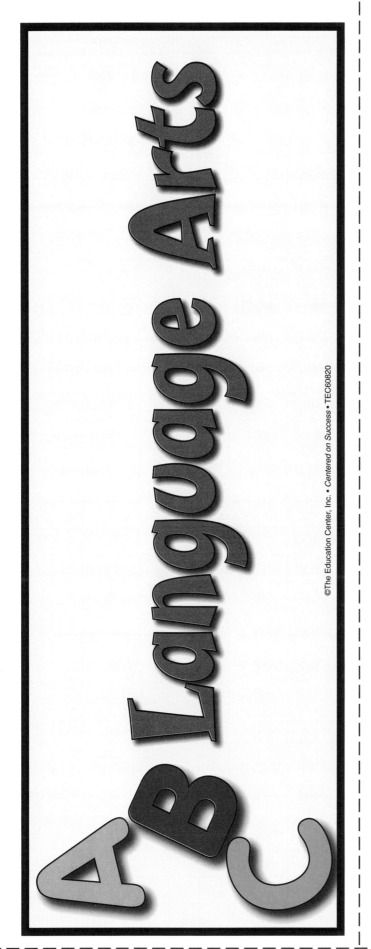

©The Education Center, Inc. • *Centered on Success* • TEC60820

©The Education Center, Inc. • *Centered on Success* • TEC60820

Note to the teacher: Tear out this page; then laminate it if desired. Cut out the labels and post the appropriate one at your yellow center.

5

Center Checklist

Center Title

Student Name											
1.											
2.											
3.											
4.											
5.											
6.											
7.											
8.											
9.											
10.											
11.											
12.											
13.											
14.											
15.											
16.											
17.											
18.											
19.											
20.											
21.											
22.											
23.											
24.											
25.											
26.											
27.											
28.											
29.											
30.											

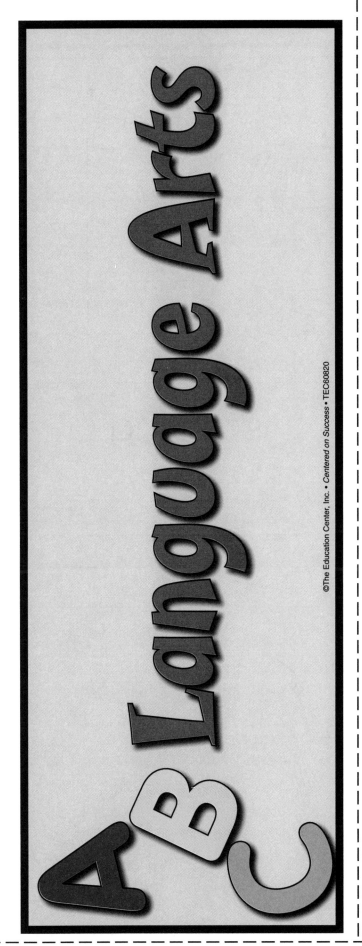

©The Education Center, Inc. • *Centered on Success* • TEC60820

©The Education Center, Inc. • *Centered on Success* • TEC60820

Note to the teacher: Tear out this page; then laminate it if desired. Cut out the labels and post the appropriate one at your blue center.

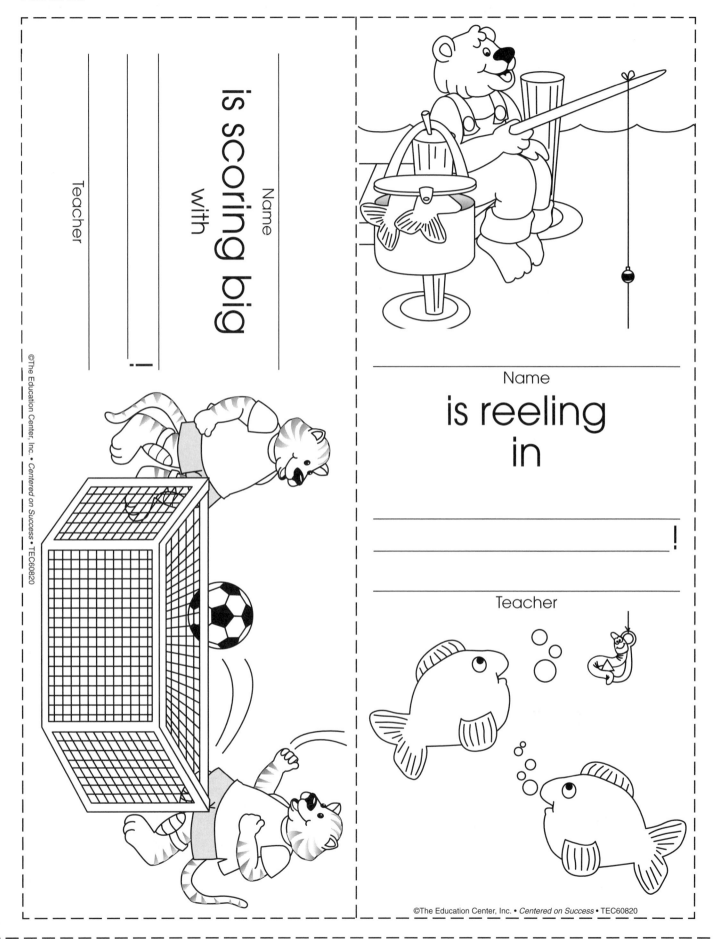

is scoring big
with

Name

Teacher

is reeling
in

Name

Teacher

Note to the teacher: Duplicate an award for each child. Personalize and distribute these awards when appropriate.

Mussel Beach

 Beginning consonants *f, m,* and *s*

 Beginning consonants *k, p,* and *r*

Materials:
- center mat on page 11
- activity cards on page 13
- activity cards on page 15
- 2 resealable plastic bags

Preparing the centers:
1. Laminate the center mat and cards.
2. Cut three slits in the center mat along the dashed lines.
3. Cut the cards apart. Put each set into a separate bag.
4. Place the bags and center mat at a center.

Using the centers:
1. A student removes the cards from the bag.
2. She lays each card faceup in the center area.
3. She places a different letter card in each slit on the center mat.
4. She names a picture card and identifies the beginning consonant.
5. She turns the card over to check her answer. If her answer is correct, she places the card on the top shell of the matching mussel. If her answer is incorrect, she repeats the name of the picture and then identifies the letter correctly before placing it on the matching mussel.
6. She repeats Steps 4–6 until each card is placed on the correct mussel.

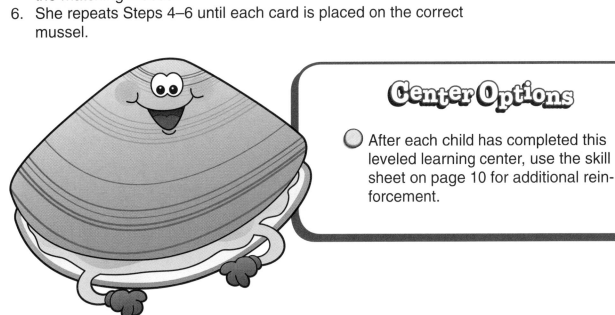

Center Options

- After each child has completed this leveled learning center, use the skill sheet on page 10 for additional reinforcement.

Name_____ *Beginning consonants k, r, and p*

A Pile of Pearls

 Color by the code.

©The Education Center, Inc. • *Centered on Success* • TEC60820

Mussel Beach

1. Choose a card.
2. Say the name of the picture.
3. Say the beginning letter.
4. Check. If correct, put the card on the matching shell.

___ ug   ___ ask   ___ oon   ___ ouse

___ an   ___ ence   ___ ish   ___ ive

___ un   ___ eal   ___ oap   ___ ock

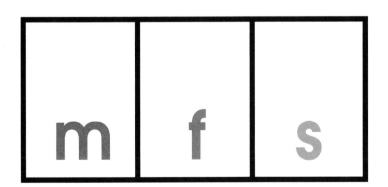

m   f   s

mouse	moon	mask	mug
five	fish	fence	fan
sock	soap	seal	sun

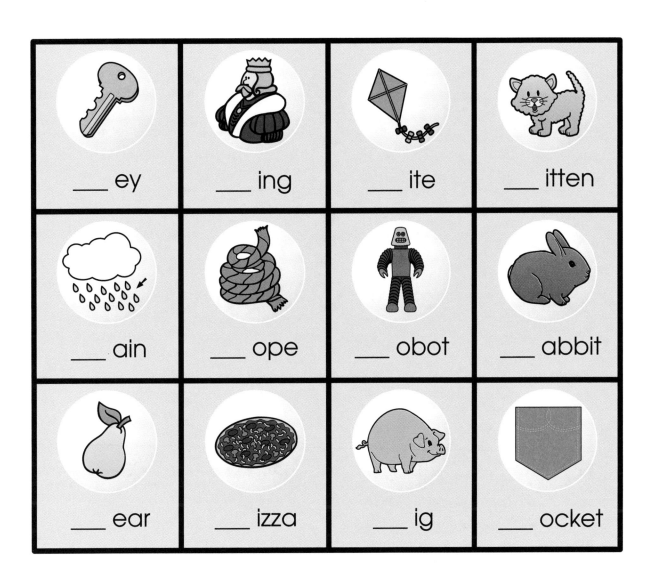

___ ey ___ ing ___ ite ___ itten

___ ain ___ ope ___ obot ___ abbit

___ ear ___ izza ___ ig ___ ocket

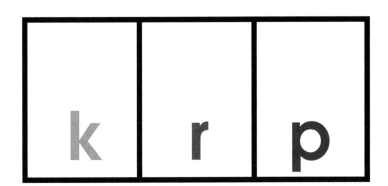

k r p

kitten	kite	king	key
rabbit	robot	rope	rain
pocket	pig	pizza	pear

Play Ball!

 Identifying short-vowel sounds /a/ and /i/

 Identifying short-vowel sounds /a/, /e/, /i/, /o/, and /u/

Materials:

center mat on page 19
○ activity cards on page 21
○ activity cards on page 23
2 resealable plastic bags

Preparing the center:

1. Laminate the center mat, balls, and cards if desired.
2. Cut out the balls and cards. Put each set into a separate bag.
3. Place the bags and center mat at a center.

Using the center:

1. A student removes the cards from the bag.
2. He lays each card faceup in the center area.
3. He places a ball on the seal where indicated and says its sound.
4. He finds the picture cards with the matching short-vowel sound.
5. He turns the cards over to check his answers. If his answers match, he places the ball in the bag and returns the cards (faceup) to the center area. If his answers do not match, he places the picture card(s) with the remaining cards and repeats Step 4.
6. He repeats Steps 3–5 until each ball has been placed in the bag.

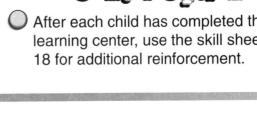

Center Option

○ After each child has completed this leveled learning center, use the skill sheet on page 18 for additional reinforcement.

Having a Ball!

Color each ball by the code.

ă—orange
ĕ—yellow
ĭ—green
ŏ—blue
ŭ—red

Note to the teacher: Use with "Play Ball" on page 17.

Play Ball!

1. Choose a ball.
2. Say the sound.
3. Match the cards with the sound.
4. Check. If correct, put the ball in the bag.

c_ _t

f_ _sh

b_ _g

p_ _g

h_ _t

w_ _g

m_ _t

b_ _b

m_ _p

p_ _n

fish	cat
pig	bag
wig	hat
bib	mat
pin	map

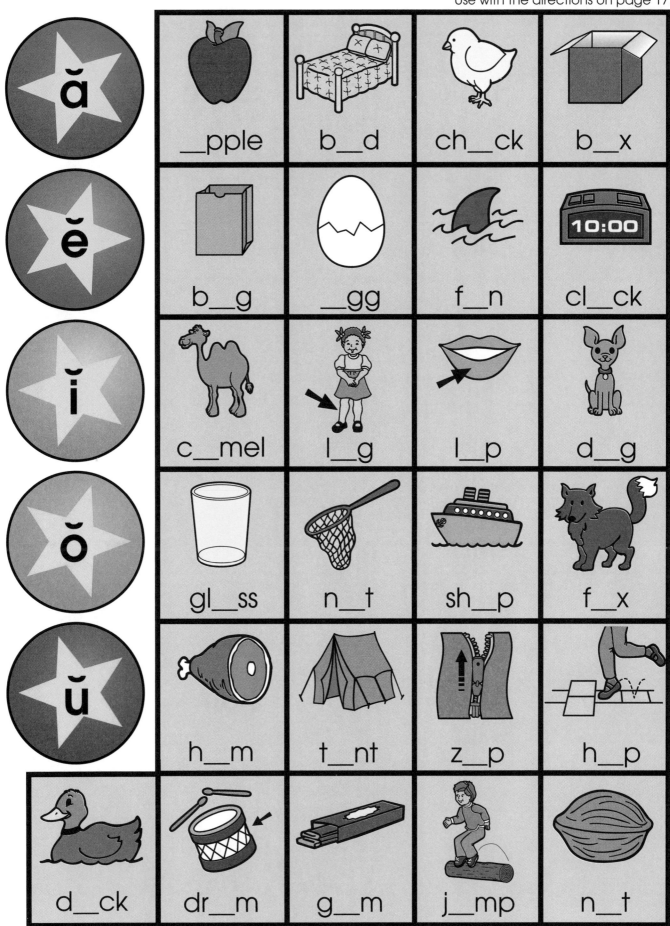

ă

ě

ĭ

ŏ

ŭ

__pple | b__d | ch__ck | b__x

b__g | __gg | f__n | cl__ck

c__mel | l__g | l__p | d__g

gl__ss | n__t | sh__p | f__x

h__m | t__nt | z__p | h__p

d__ck | dr__m | g__m | j__mp | n__t

box   chick   bed   apple

clock   fin   egg   bag

dog   lip   leg   camel

fox   ship   net   glass

hop   zip   tent   ham

nut   jump   gum   drum   duck

Gone Fishin'

 Identifying long-vowel sounds /a/ and /i/

 Identifying long-vowel sounds /a/, /e/, /i/, /o/, and /u/

Materials:

center mat on page 27
activity cards on page 29
activity cards on page 31
paper clip
2 resealable plastic bags

Preparing the centers:

1. Laminate the center mat, baskets, and cards.
2. Cut a slit along the dashed line on the center mat. Attach a paper clip.
3. Cut out the baskets and cards. Put each set into a separate bag.
4. Place the bags and center mat at a center.

Using the centers:

1. A student removes the cards from the bag.
2. She lays each card faceup in the center area.
3. She chooses a basket card, clips it to the center mat, and says its sound.
4. She finds a picture card with a matching vowel sound.
5. She turns the card over to check her answer. If her answer matches, she places the card on a fish on the center mat. If her answer does not match, she places the card with the remaining activity cards.
6. She repeats Steps 4–5 until she has covered all the fish.
7. She puts the basket card in the bag. She places the picture cards faceup in the center area.
8. She repeats Steps 3–7 with each remaining basket card.

Center Option

After each child has completed this leveled learning center, use the skill sheet on page 26 for additional reinforcement.

Name _____

26

Big Catch

✏ Write **a**, **e**, **i**, **o**, or **u** to finish each word.

🖍 Color by the code.

Color Code

a—red   o—green
e—yellow u—orange
i—blue

b__ke

h__se

k__y

m__ce

m__le

t__pe

c__at

v__se

c__be

Note to the teacher: Use with "Gone Fishin'" on page 25.

Gone Fishin'

1. Put a basket card on the mat.
2. Say the vowel sound.
3. Find a picture card with the matching vowel sound.
4. Check. If correct, put the card on a fish.

©The Education Center, Inc. • Centered on Success • TEC60820

27

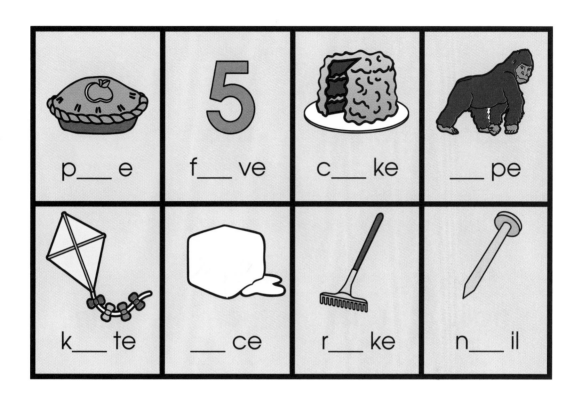

p___e   f__ve   c___ke   ___pe

k___te   ___ce   r___ke   n___il

ā   ī

ā
ape

ā
cake

ī
five

ī
pie

ā
nail

ā
rake

ī
ice

ī
kite

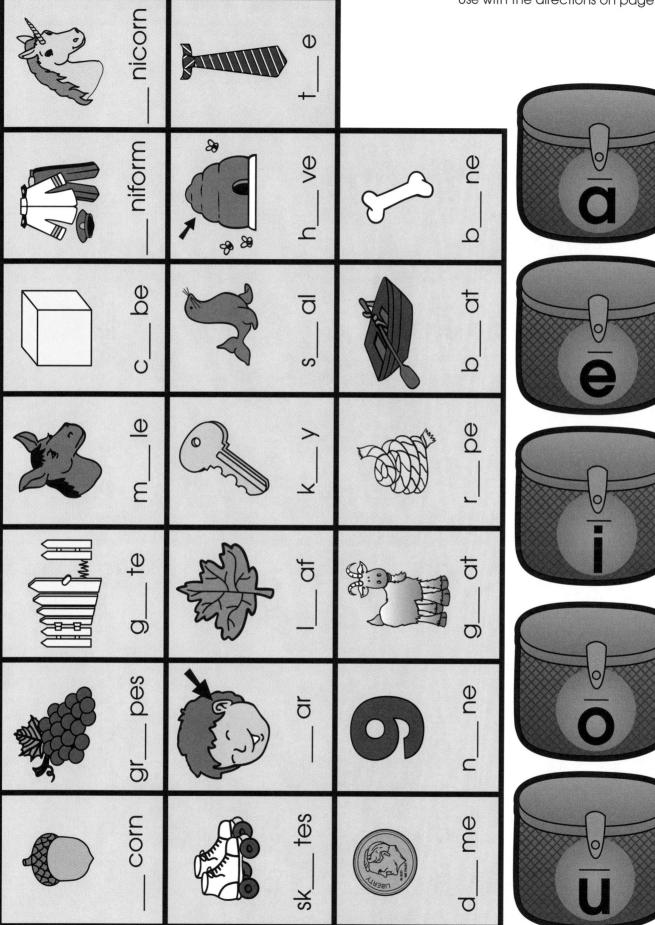

___ nicorn

t___e

___ niform

h___ve

b___ne

c___be

s___al

b___at

m___le

k___y

r___pe

g___te

l___af

g___at

gr___pes

___ar

9

n___ne

___ corn

sk___tes

d___me

ā

ē

ī

ō

u

ū unicorn ū uniform ū cube ū mule ā gate ā grapes ā acorn

ī tie ī hive ē seal ē key ē leaf ē ear ā skates

ō bone ō boat ō rope ō goat ī nine ī dime

Goal Kicks

 Identifying ending sounds /l/, /m/, and /t/

 Identifying ending sounds /d/, /g/, and /p/

Materials:
- center mat on page 35
- ○ activity cards on page 37
- ◔ activity cards on page 39
- 3 paper clips
- 2 resealable plastic bags

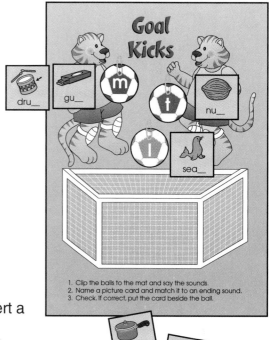

Preparing the centers:
1. Laminate the center mat, balls, and cards.
2. Cut slits along the dashed lines on the center mat. Insert a paper clip in each slit.
3. Cut out the balls and cards. Put each set into a separate bag.
4. Place the bags and center mat at a center.

Using the centers:
1. A student removes the cards from the bag.
2. He places each card faceup in the center area.
3. He clips each ball to the mat where indicated and says its sound.
4. He names a picture card, listens for its ending sound, and decides which of the balls it matches.
5. He turns the card over to check his answer. If his answer is correct, he places the card beside the matching ball. If his answer is incorrect, he places the card with the remaining activity cards.
6. He repeats Steps 4–5 until he has matched each set of cards to the appropriate ball.

Center Option
○ After each child has completed this leveled learning center, use the reproducible skill sheet on page 34 for additional reinforcement.

Soccer Practice

Name each picture. Listen for the ending sound.

 Write the letter.

Color.

 do___

 fro___

 cu___

 fla___

 sa___

 to___

 han___

 pi___

 sto___

be___

Bonus Box: On the back of this sheet, write three words that end with /t/.

Goal Kicks

1. Clip the balls to the mat and say the sounds.
2. Name a picture card and match it to an ending sound.
3. Check. If correct, put the card beside the ball.

sea__   po__   dru__

pai__   nu__   ja__

penci__   ne__   ha__

came__   ba__   gu__

drum	pot	seal
jam	nut	pail
ham	net	pencil
gum	bat	camel

yar__   shee__   ru__

sle__   li__   fla__

clou__   ho__   lo__

be__   ca__   wi__

rug   sheep   yard

flag   lip   sled

log   hop   cloud

wig   cap   bed

Ferris Wheel Fun

 Matching rhyming words and pictures (pairs)

 Matching rhyming words and pictures (trios)

Materials:
- center mat on page 43
- activity cards on page 45
- activity cards on page 47
- 2 resealable plastic bags

Preparing the centers:
1. Laminate the center mat and cards if desired.
2. Cut out the cards. Put each set into a separate bag.
3. Place the bags and center mat at a center.

Using the centers:
1. A student removes the cards from the bag.
2. She places each card faceup in the center area.
3. She chooses a card and finds a rhyming picture card or cards.
4. She turns over each card to check her answer. If her answer matches, she places the card on the center mat. If her answer does not match, she places the card with the remaining activity cards.
5. She repeats Steps 3–5 until she has placed each set of cards on the ferris wheel.

Center Option

After each child has completed this leveled learning center, use the reproducible skill sheet on page 42 for additional reinforcement.

Sky-High Rhymes

✂ Cut.
△ Match.
🧴 Glue.

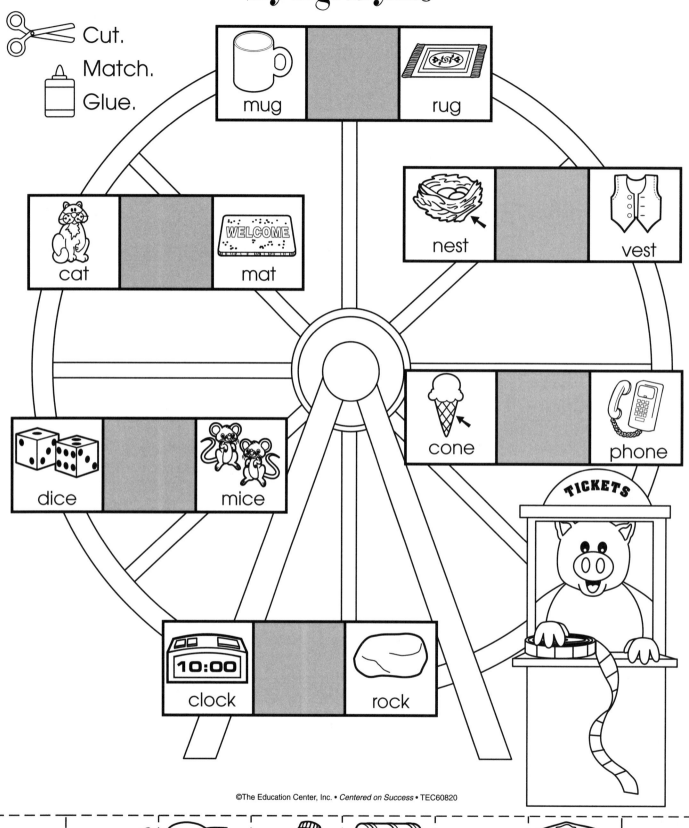

bat   plug   sock   chest   bone   ice

©The Education Center, Inc. • *Centered on Success* • TEC60820

Ferris Wheel Fun

TICKETS

1. Choose a card.
2. Say the word.
3. Find a card or cards that rhyme.
4. Check. If correct, put the cards on the Ferris wheel.

©The Education Center, Inc. • Centered on Success • TEC60820

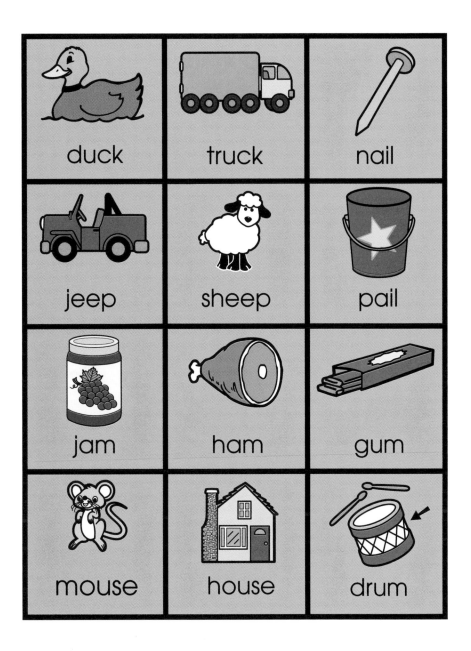

duck	truck	nail
jeep	sheep	pail
jam	ham	gum
mouse	house	drum

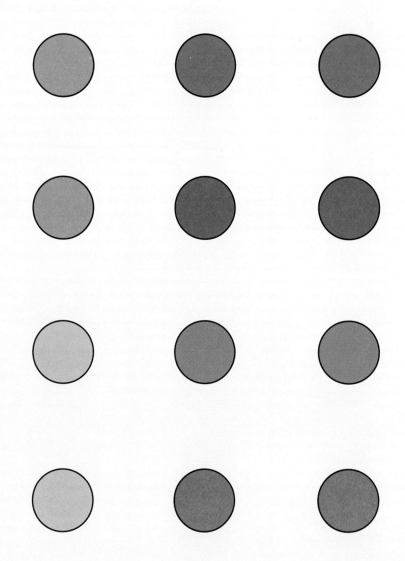

plug mug rug

can pan man

dice mice ice

nest vest chest

sock rock clock

cake rake snake

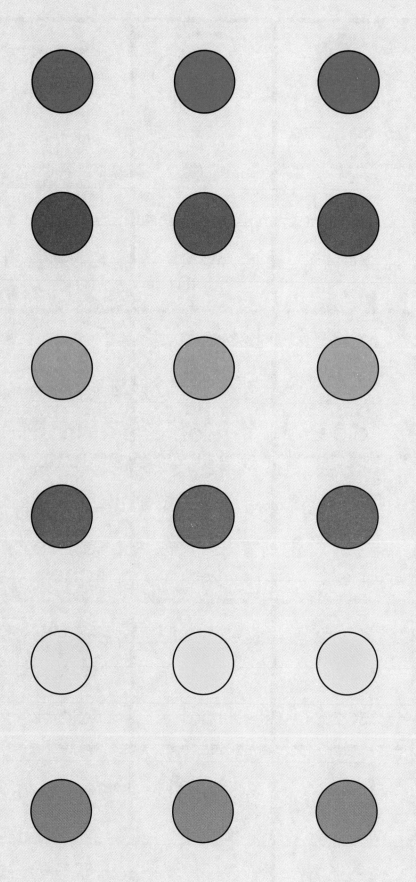

Blowing Bubbles

 Identifying word families with pictures: *-an, -ape*

 Identifying word families with pictures and words: *-at, -ake*

Materials:
center mat on page 51
⬜ activity cards on page 53
⬜ activity cards on page 55
2 resealable plastic bags

Preparing the centers:
1. Laminate the center mat and cards if desired.
2. Cut the cards apart. Put each set into a separate bag.
3. Place the bags and center mat at a center.

Using the centers:
1. A student removes the cards from the bag.
2. She lays each card faceup in the center area.
3. She places each large picture card on a different bubble on the center mat.
4. She names a small picture card and places it below the large card from the same word family.
⬜ She places the word card next to the picture card.
5. She repeats Step 4 until each card has been placed on the center mat.
6. She turns the cards over to check her answers. If her answers are correct, she places the cards back in the bag. If her answers are incorrect, she rearranges the cards to make word families and then continues in this same manner.

Center Option
⬜ After each child has completed this leveled learning center, use the skill sheet on page 50 for additional reinforcement.

49

Bubbles All Around!

Color by the code.

Color Code

-at   green
-ake   blue
-an   red
-ape   orange

Bonus Box: Choose five pictures. On the back of this page, write the names of the pictures.

Blowing Bubbles

1. Choose a card.
2. Say the name of its picture.
3. Place the card under the word family bubble.
4. Repeat with each card.
5. Check.

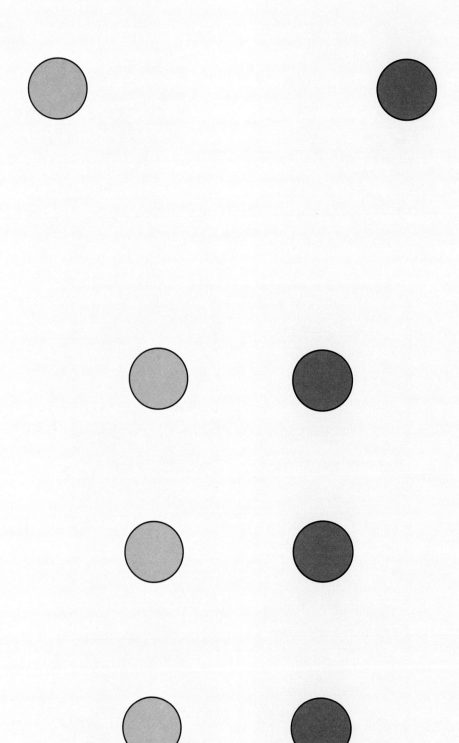

cat	rake
bat	snake
mat	flake

cat   rake

bat   snake

mat   flake

                    rake   cat

                    mat   snake

                    flake   mat

Movin' On

 Sequencing three sentences

 Sequencing four sentences

Materials:
center mat on page 59
◯ activity cards on page 61
◯ activity cards on page 63
2 resealable plastic bags

Preparing the centers:
1. Laminate the center mat and cards if desired.
2. Cut the cards apart. Put each set into a separate bag.
3. Place the bags and center mat at a center.

Using the centers:
1. A student removes the cards from the bag.
2. She lays the cards faceup in the center area.
3. She sorts the cards into sets.
4. She reads each card in one set.
5. She arranges the cards in sequential order on the truck.
6. She turns the cards over to check her answers. If her answers are correct, she puts that set of cards in the bag. If her answers are incorrect, she arranges the cards.
7. She repeats Steps 4–6 for each remaining set of cards.

Center Options

◯ If desired, have each child write each sentence on a separate sheet of paper and then illustrate each one.

◯ After each child has completed this leveled learning center, use the skill sheet on page 58 for additional reinforcement.

57

Name _____

Load Them Up!

Read each sentence. 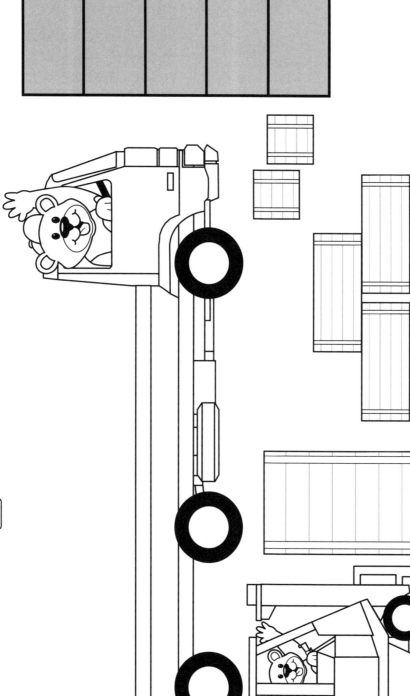 Glue the sentences in order. Color.

©The Education Center, Inc. • *Centered on Success* • TEC60820

The truck was full.

Next, they put on three blue boxes.

Finally, they put on two yellow boxes.

First, they loaded one red box.

One day, I saw workers load a truck.

Note to the teacher: Use with "Movin' On" on page 57.

Movin' On

1. Sort the cards by color.
2. Read the cards in one set.
3. Place the cards in order on the truck.
4. Check.
5. Play again with a new set of cards.

I got out of bed.	I ate fruit and milk.	I brushed my teeth after I ate.
I put on my swimsuit.	I got into the water.	I splashed my mom.
I put on my coat and hat.	I ran outside to play.	I came in for a snack.

3   2   1

3   2   1

3   2   1

I took a bath.

I helped Dad make lunch.

I put on my pajamas.

We cooked hot dogs.

I got into bed.

Dad put a hot dog on my plate.

I went to sleep.

We ate lunch.

1   1

2   2

3   3

4   4

Choo-Choo Choices

Using ending punctuation: period and question mark

Using ending punctuation: period, question mark, and exclamation mark

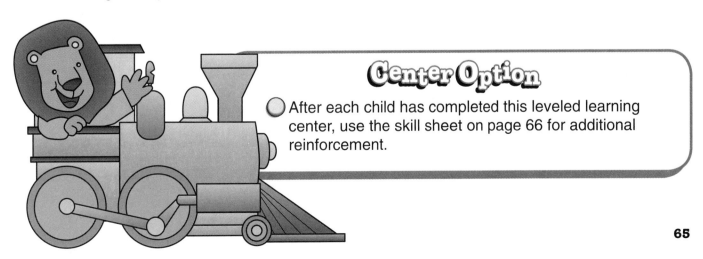

Materials:
- center mat on page 67
- activity cards on page 69
- activity cards on page 71
- 2 resealable plastic bags

Preparing the center:
1. Laminate the center mat and cards if desired.
2. Cut out the caboose cards and cut the sentence cards apart. Put each set into a separate bag.
3. Place the bags and center mat at a center.

Using the center:
1. A student removes the cards from the bag.
2. He places the sentence cards and caboose cards faceup in the center area.
3. He chooses a sentence card and places it in the space provided on the train.
4. He reads the sentence.
5. He decides which ending punctuation completes the sentence and then places the corresponding caboose card on the mat.
6. He turns the sentence card over to check his answer. If his answer matches, he places the sentence card in the bag and puts the caboose card back in the center area. If his answer does not match, he places both cards with the remaining activity cards and continues in this same manner.

Center Option
After each child has completed this leveled learning center, use the skill sheet on page 66 for additional reinforcement.

Name _____

Chuggin' Along

Read each sentence.

✏️ Write . or ? or ! in each ☐.

🖍️ Color a matching car as you go.

1. Will the train be late ☐

2. The horn is too loud ☐

3. Get on the train quickly ☐

4. When will the train stop ☐

5. Are you sure it's on time ☐

6. The train has many wheels ☐

7. Take your seat now ☐

8. Take the second train ☐

9. I will return on the train ☐

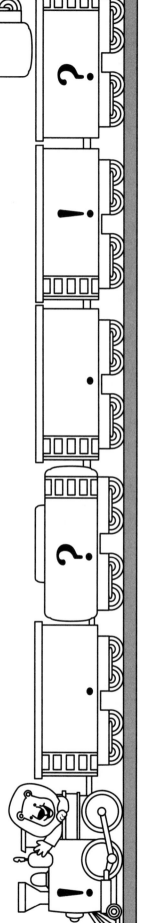

©The Education Center, Inc. • Centered on Success • TEC60820

Note to the teacher: Use with "Choo-Choo Choices" on page 65.

Choo-Choo Choices

1. Put a sentence card on the train.
2. Read the sentence.
3. Put the matching caboose on the train.
4. Check. If correct, put the sentence card in the bag.
   Put the caboose back in the center area.
5. Play again with another set of cards.

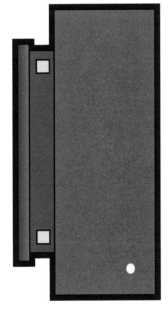

Did you ride with a friend	Do you have any bags	How was your trip
Why is the train late	How long can you stay	Where did you get on the train
I ate lunch on the train	I rode with Sam	The ride was nice
We rode all day	I sat with my mother	The train is big

? question mark

? question mark

? question mark

? question mark

? question mark

? question mark

. period

. period

. period

. period

. period

. period

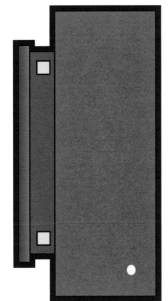

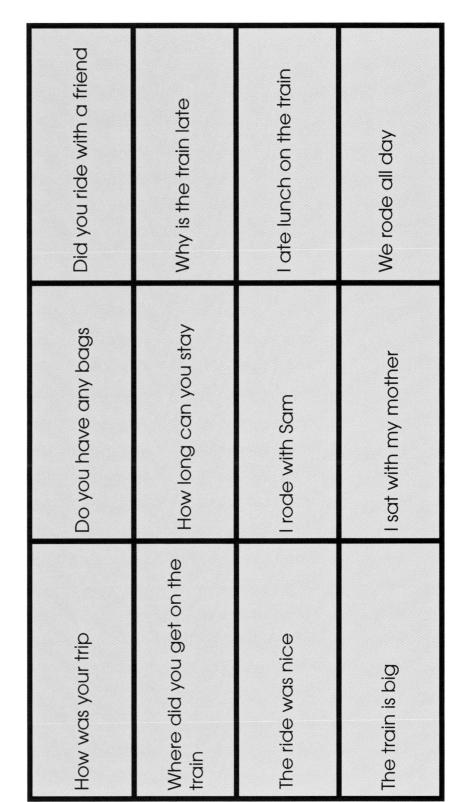

Did you ride with a friend

Why is the train late

I ate lunch on the train

We rode all day

Do you have any bags

How long can you stay

I rode with Sam

I sat with my mother

How was your trip

Where did you get on the train

The ride was nice

The train is big

? question mark

? question mark

? question mark

? question mark

? question mark

? question mark

. period

. period

. period

. period

. period

. period

The train is so fast	Wow, what a fun ride	The train is too hot
I like the train	We rode the train together	The train ride will be quick
Did you ride the train today	My friend went home on the train	The train is early
When is the train coming	May I sit with you on the train	Who is on the train

! exclamation mark   ! exclamation mark   ! exclamation mark

. period   . period   . period

? question mark   ? question mark   ? question mark

? question mark   ? question mark   ? question mark

Finned Friends

 Capitalizing the first word in a sentence

 Capitalizing the first word in a sentence, names, days of the week, and months

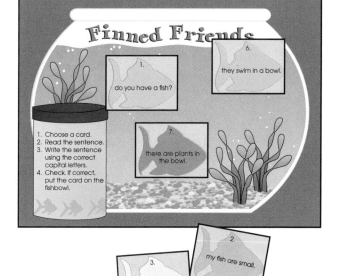

Materials:

supply of the recording sheet on page 74
center mat on page 75
activity cards on page 77
activity cards on page 79
2 resealable plastic bags

Preparing the centers:

1. Laminate the center mat and cards if desired.
2. Cut the cards apart. Put each set into a separate bag.
3. Place the bags, center mat, and copies of the recording sheet at a center.

Using the centers:

1. A student removes the cards from the bag.
2. She places each card faceup in the center area.
3. She chooses a card and reads the sentence.
4. She writes the sentence on the recording sheet, changing lowercase letters to capitals where needed.
5. She turns the card over to check her answer. If her sentence is correct, she places the card on the fish bowl. If her sentence is not correct, she makes the needed changes before placing the card on the bowl.
6. She repeats Steps 3–5, correcting the sentences until each card is placed on the bowl.

Center Option

If desired, invite pairs of students to work in the center together. A student chooses a card and writes the corrected sentence on a shared recording sheet. The partner checks and confirms the corrected sentence, then takes a turn.

Name _____

Finned Friends

1. _____

2. _____

3. _____

4. _____

5. _____

6. _____

7. _____

8. _____

Note to the teacher: Use with "Finned Friends" on page 73.

Finned Friends

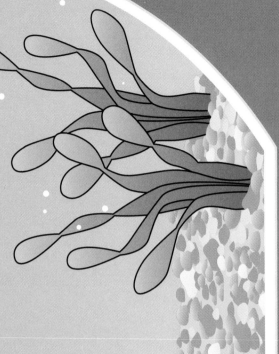

1. Choose a card.
2. Read the sentence.
3. Write the sentence using the correct capital letters.
4. Check. If correct, put the card on the fishbowl.

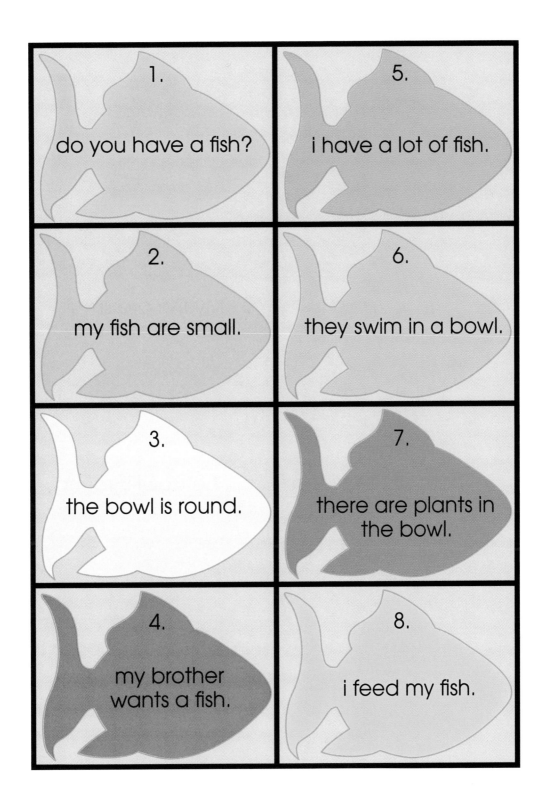

1. do you have a fish?

2. my fish are small.

3. the bowl is round.

4. my brother wants a fish.

5. i have a lot of fish.

6. they swim in a bowl.

7. there are plants in the bowl.

8. i feed my fish.

5. I have a lot of fish.

1. Do you have a fish?

6. They swim in a bowl.

2. My fish are small.

7. There are plants in the bowl.

3. The bowl is round.

8. I feed my fish.

4. My brother wants a fish.

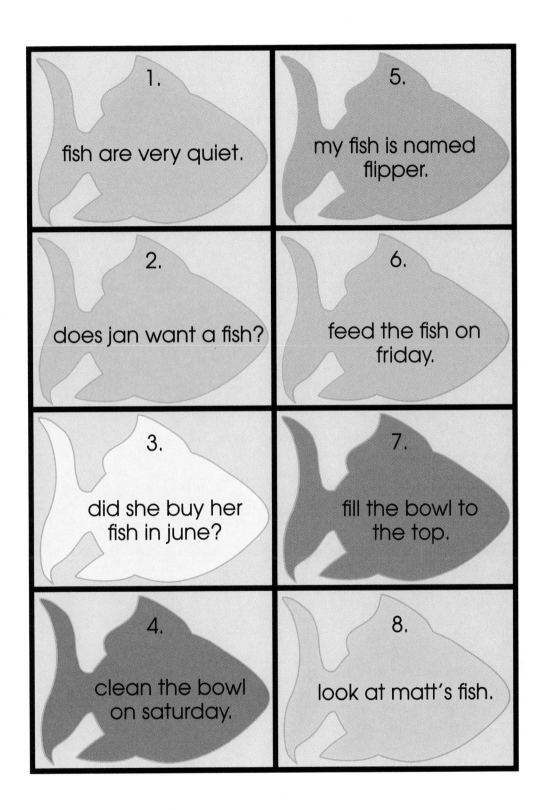

1.
fish are very quiet.

2.
does jan want a fish?

3.
did she buy her fish in june?

4.
clean the bowl on saturday.

5.
my fish is named flipper.

6.
feed the fish on friday.

7.
fill the bowl to the top.

8.
look at matt's fish.

5. My fish is named
   Flipper.

1. Fish are very
   quiet.

6. Feed the fish on
   Friday.

2. Does Jan want a
   fish?

7. Fill the bowl to the
   top.

3. Did she buy her
   fish in June?

8. Look at Matt's fish.

4. Clean the bowl
   on Saturday.

Flutter and Fly

 Alphabetizing three words

 Alphabetizing five words

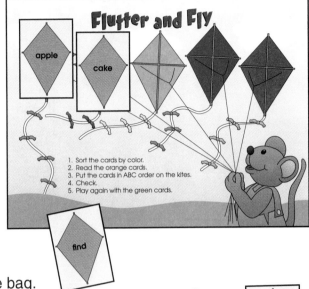

Materials:
- center mat on page 83
- activity cards on page 85
- activity cards on page 87
- 2 resealable plastic bags

Preparing the centers:
1. Laminate the center mat and cards if desired.
2. Cut the cards apart. Put each set into a separate bag.
3. Place the bags and center mat at a center.

Using the centers:
1. A student removes the cards from the bag.
2. He lays the cards faceup in the center area.
3. He sorts the orange cards and reads them.
4. He arranges the cards in ABC order and puts each card on a different kite (in order) on the center mat.
5. He turns the cards over to check his answers. If his answers are correct, he puts the cards in the bag. If his answers are incorrect, he rearranges the cards.
6. He repeats Steps 4–5 with the green cards.

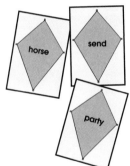

Center Options

- If desired, challenge a pair of students to mix all the blue level cards together and then arrange them in ABC order.

- After each child has completed this leveled learning center, use the skill sheet on page 82 for additional reinforcement.

Soaring High

Read the words on one kite.

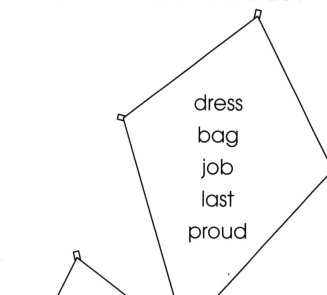 Write the words in ABC order.

dress
bag
job
last
proud

1. _____

2. _____

3. _____

4. _____

5. _____

make
town
kind
write
shoe

1. _____

2. _____

3. _____

4. _____

5. _____

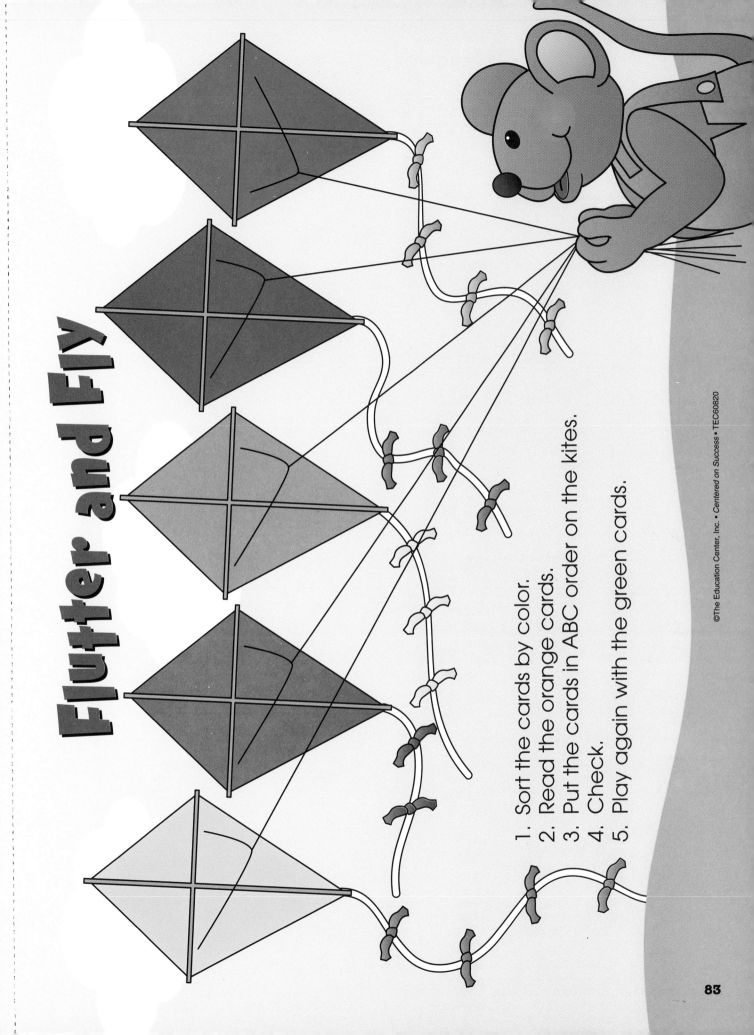

Flutter and Fly

1. Sort the cards by color.
2. Read the orange cards.
3. Put the cards in ABC order on the kites.
4. Check.
5. Play again with the green cards.

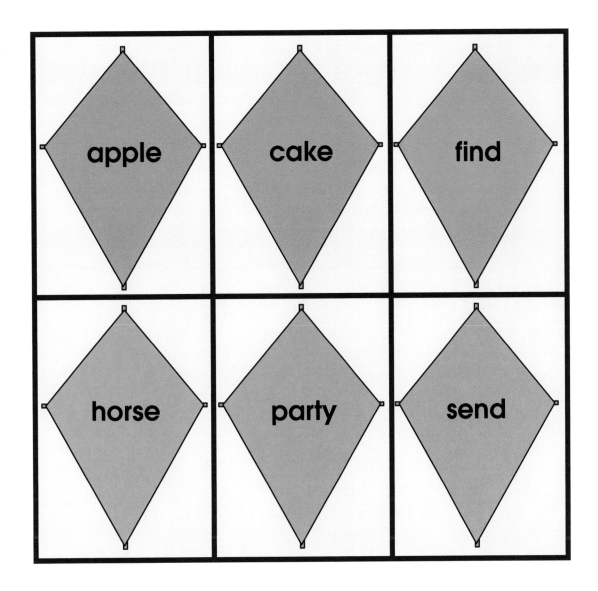

3   2   1

3   2   1

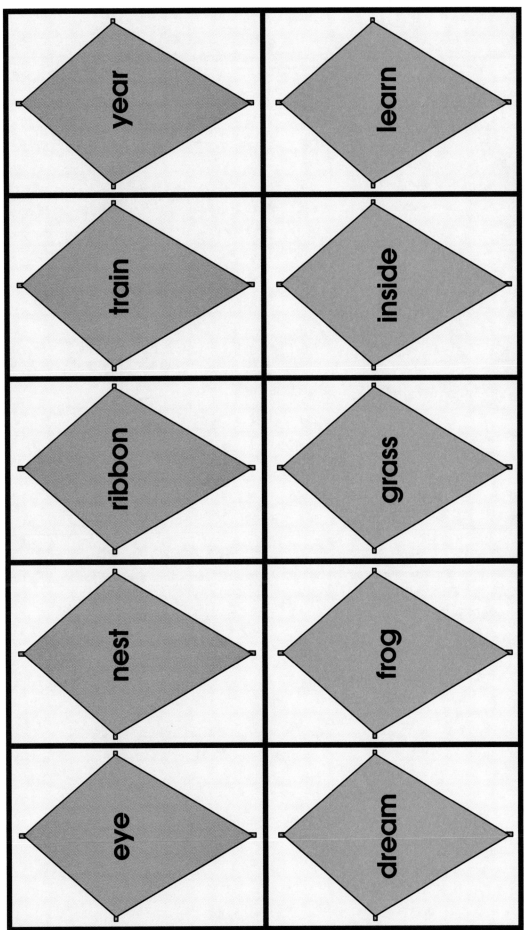

year

learn

train

inside

ribbon

grass

nest

frog

eye

dream

5

5

4

4

3

3

2

2

1

1

Count the Stars

 Sequencing numbers 1–50

 Sequencing numbers 1–100

Count the Stars

c) 24, 25, ___, 27

1	2	3	4	5	6	7	8	9	10
11	12	13	14	15	16	17	18	19	20
21	22	23	24	25	26	27	28	29	30
31	32	33	34	35	36	37	38	39	40
41	42	43	44	45	46	47	48	49	50
51	52	53	54	55	56	57	58	59	60
61	62	63	64	65	66	67	68	69	70
71	72	73	74	75	76	77	78	79	80
81	82	83	84	85	86	87	88	89	90
91	92	93	94	95	96	97	98	99	100

1. Choose a card.
2. Think about the missing numbers.
3. Write all the numbers on your recording sheet.
4. Check. If correct, put the card on the box.

Materials:

supply of the recording sheet on page 90
center mat on page 91
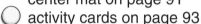activity cards on page 93
activity cards on page 95
2 resealable plastic bags

Preparing the centers:

1. Laminate the center mat and cards if desired.
2. Cut the cards apart. Put each set into a separate bag.
3. Place the bags, center mat, and copies of the recording sheet at a center.

Using the centers:

1. A student removes the cards from the bag.
2. He lays the cards faceup in the center area.
3. He chooses a card and determines the missing numbers in the set.
4. He writes the number set on his recording sheet.
5. He turns the card over to check his answer. If his answer is correct, he places the card in the box on the center mat. If his answer is incorrect, he corrects his recording sheet and then places the card in the box on the center mat.
6. He continues in this manner with the remaining cards.

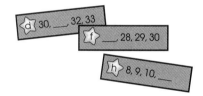

d) 30, ___, 32, 33

f) ___, 28, 29, 30

h) 8, 9, 10, ___

Center Options

After each child has completed this leveled learning center, have him put the activity cards in order for additional reinforcement.

89

Count the Stars

a ___ — ___ — ___ — ___

b ___ — ___ — ___ — ___

c ___ — ___ — ___ — ___

d ___ — ___ — ___ — ___

e ___ — ___ — ___ — ___

f ___ — ___ — ___ — ___

g ___ — ___ — ___ — ___

h ___ — ___ — ___ — ___

i ___ — ___ — ___ — ___

j ___ — ___ — ___ — ___

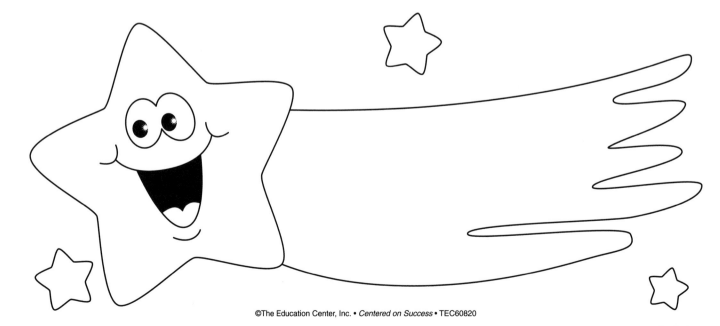

Count the Stars

1	2	3	4	5	6	7	8	9	10
11	12	13	14	15	16	17	18	19	20
21	22	23	24	25	26	27	28	29	30
31	32	33	34	35	36	37	38	39	40
41	42	43	44	45	46	47	48	49	50
51	52	53	54	55	56	57	58	59	60
61	62	63	64	65	66	67	68	69	70
71	72	73	74	75	76	77	78	79	80
81	82	83	84	85	86	87	88	89	90
91	92	93	94	95	96	97	98	99	100

1. Choose a card.
2. Think about the missing numbers.
3. Write all the numbers on your recording sheet.
4. Check. If correct, put the card on the box.

a ___, 3, 4, 5	f ___, 28, 29, 30
b 15, ___, 17, 18	g 43, 44, 45, ___
c 24, 25, ___, 27	h 8, 9, 10, ___
d 30, ___, 32, 33	i 39, 40, ___, 42
e 18, ___, 20, 21	j 47, 48, 49, ___

f 27, 28, 29, 30

 g 43, 44, 45, 46

 h 8, 9, 10, 11

 i 39, 40, 41, 42

 j 47, 48, 49, 50

a 2, 3, 4, 5

b 15, 16, 17, 18

 c 24, 25, 26, 27

 d 30, 31, 32, 33

e 18, 19, 20, 21

a) 4, ___, ___, 7

b) 13, ___, 15, ___

c) ___, 28, ___, 30

d) 97, ___, ___, 100

e) ___, ___, 94, 95

f) 46, ___, 48, ___

g) 55, ___, ___, 58

h) ___, 65, ___, 67

i) 76, ___, 78, ___

j) ___, 81, ___, 83

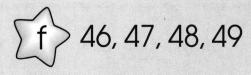 46, 47, 48, 49

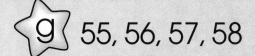 4, 5, 6, 7

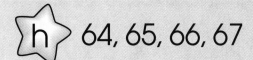 55, 56, 57, 58

13, 14, 15, 16

64, 65, 66, 67

27, 28, 29, 30

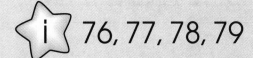 76, 77, 78, 79

97, 98, 99, 100

 80, 81, 82, 83

92, 93, 94, 95

Piggy Pancakes

 Adding sets to 5

 Adding sets to 10

Materials:

center mat on page 99
 activity cards on page 101
activity cards on page 103
2 resealable plastic bags

Preparing the centers:

1. Laminate the center mat and cards if desired.
2. Cut the cards apart. Put each set into a separate bag.
3. Place the bags and center sheet at a center.

Using the centers:

1. A student removes the cards from the bag.
2. She lays each card faceup in the center area, separating the problem cards from the manipulatives.
3. She chooses a problem card and adds the sets, using the manipulatives if needed.
4. She turns the card over to check her answer. If her answer is correct, she places the card on the pancake stack on the center mat. If her answer is incorrect, she uses the manipulatives to add the sets again.
5. She repeats Steps 3–4 until each card is placed on the pancake stack.

Center Options

If desired, place a plastic spatula at the center. Have each student use the spatula to place each completed card on the pancake stack.

After each child has completed this leveled learning center, use the skill sheet on page 98 for additional reinforcement.

Stacks of Flap Jacks!

✏️ Write how many in each set.
   Add.

[ ] + [ ] = [ ]

[ ] + [ ] = [ ]

[ ] + [ ] = [ ]

[ ] + [ ] = [ ]

[ ] + [ ] = [ ]

[ ] + [ ] = [ ]

[ ] + [ ] = [ ]

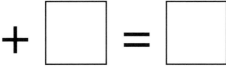

[ ] + [ ] = [ ]

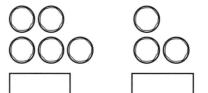

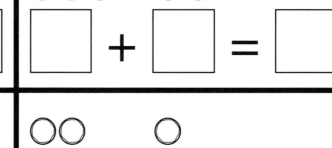

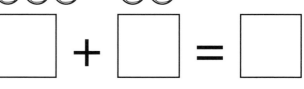

Piggy Pancakes

1. Choose a card.
2. Add the sets.
3. Check. If correct, put the card on the pancake stack.

SYRUP

©The Education Center, Inc. • *Centered on Success* • TEC60820

99

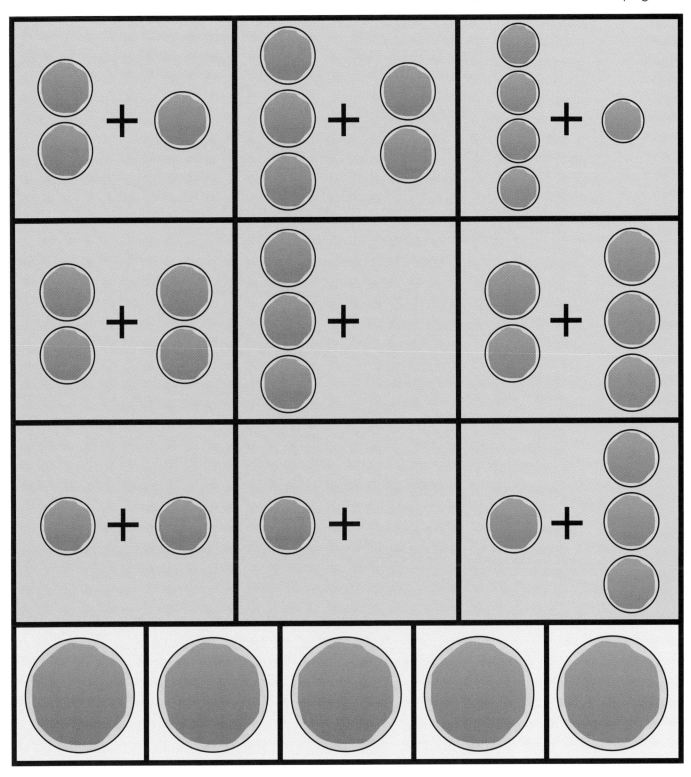

5   5   3

5   3   4

4   1   2

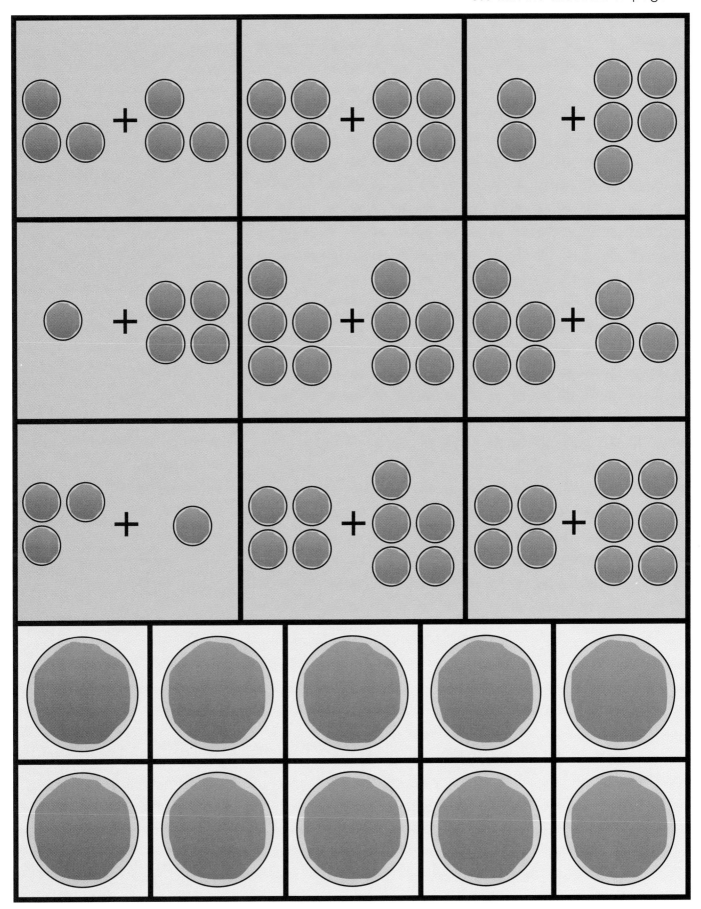

7 8 6

8 10 5

10 9 4

Fine-Feathered Friends

 Adding numbers to 5

 Adding numbers to 10

Materials:
center mat on page 107
◯ activity cards on page 109
◯ activity cards on page 111
2 resealable plastic bags

Preparing the centers:
1. Laminate the center mat and cards if desired.
2. Cut the cards apart. Put each set into a separate bag.
3. Place the bags and center mat at a center.

Using the centers:
1. A student removes the cards from the bag.
2. He lays each card faceup in the center area.
3. He chooses a problem card and reads it.
4. He uses the sunflower seed manipulatives to solve the problem if needed.
5. He turns the card over to check his answer. If his answer is correct, he places the card on the bird feeder on the center mat. If his answer is incorrect, he uses the manipulatives to add the numbers again and then continues in this same manner.
6. He repeats steps 3–5 until each card has been placed on the bird feeder.

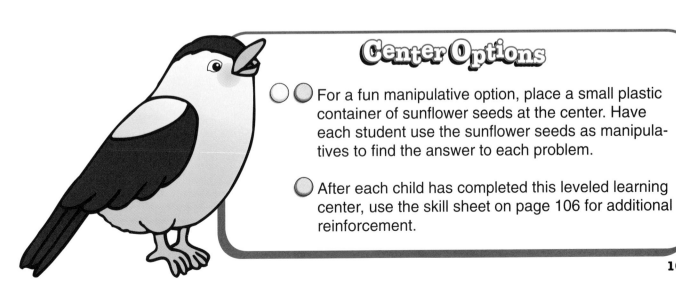

Center Options

◯ ◯ For a fun manipulative option, place a small plastic container of sunflower seeds at the center. Have each student use the sunflower seeds as manipulatives to find the answer to each problem.

◯ After each child has completed this leveled learning center, use the skill sheet on page 106 for additional reinforcement.

Birdie "Tweets"!

Add. ✏️ Write.

🖍 Color the matching seed below.

6 + 4	4 + 5	4 + 4

4 + 3	2 + 8	3 + 7

5 + 5	9 + 1	7 + 2

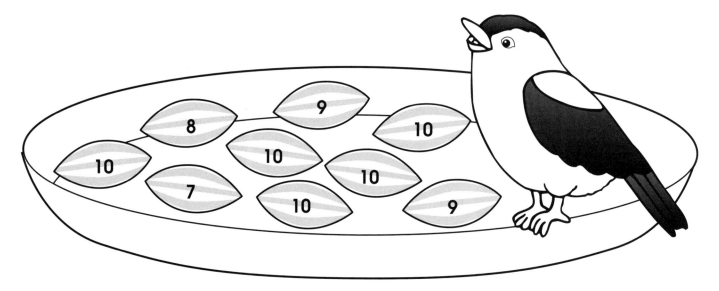

Fine-Feathered Friends

1. Choose a card.
2. Add the numbers.
3. Check. If correct, put the card on the bird feeder.

2 + 1 =	1 + 4 =	2 + 2 =
1 + 3 =	5 + 0 =	3 + 2 =
0 + 5 =	4 + 1 =	2 + 3 =

4	5	3
5	5	4
5	5	5

9 + 1 =	8 + 2 =	7 + 2 =
4 + 5 =	10 + 0 =	4 + 6 =
6 + 2 =	5 + 5 =	3 + 7 =

9   10   10

10   10   9

10   10   8

Movie Treats

 Subtracting numbers to 5

 Subtracting numbers to 10

Materials:

center mat on page 115
activity cards on page 117
activity cards on page 119
2 resealable plastic bags

Preparing the center:

1. Laminate the center mat and cards if desired.
2. Cut the cards apart. Put each set into a separate bag.
3. Place the bags and center mat at a center.

Using the center:

1. A student removes the cards from the bag.
2. He lays each card faceup in the center area.
3. He chooses a problem card and reads it.
4. He uses the manipulatives (popcorn cards) to solve the problem if needed.
5. He turns the card over to check his answer. If his answer is correct, he places the card in the box on the center sheet. If his answer is incorrect, he uses the manipulatives to subtract the numbers again and then continues in this same manner.
6. He repeats Steps 3–5 until each card has been placed on the box.

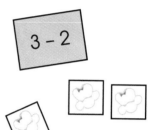

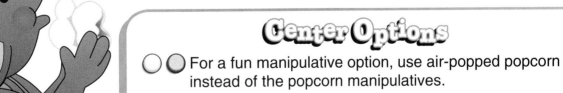

Center Options

For a fun manipulative option, use air-popped popcorn instead of the popcorn manipulatives.

After each child has completed this leveled learning center, use the skill sheet on page 114 for additional reinforcement.

Salty Snacks

Subtract.

10 – 3 = ___

10 – 4 = ___

10 – 8 = ___

10 – 6 = ___

10 – 5 = ___

10 – 0 = ___

10 – 7 = ___

10 – 1 = ___

10 – 9 = ___

10 – 2 = ___

Popcorn

©The Education Center, Inc. • Centered on Success • TEC60820

Movie Treats

1. Choose a card.
2. Read the problem.
3. Subtract.
4. Check. If correct, put the card on the box.

3 – 2	3 – 3
5 – 1	5 – 4
5 – 3	5 – 2
5 – 0	5 – 5
4 – 2	4 – 1

0   1

1   4

3   2

0   5

3   2

10 – 9	10 – 8
10 – 7	10 – 6
10 – 5	10 – 4
10 – 3	10 – 2
10 – 1	10 – 10

2   1

4   3

6   5

8   7

0   9

Kitty Toys

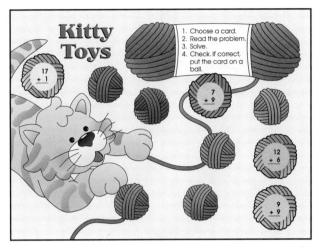

Materials:
center mat on page 123
activity cards on page 125
activity cards on page 127
2 resealable plastic bags

Preparing the center:
1. Laminate the center mat and cards if desired.
2. Cut the cards apart. Put each set into a separate bag.
3. Place the bags and center mat at a center.

Using the center:
1. A student removes the cards from the bag.
2. He lays each card faceup in the center area.
3. He chooses a problem card and reads it.
4. He uses the mouse manipulatives, if necessary, to solve the problem.
5. He turns the card over to check his answer. If his answer is correct, he places the problem card on a yarn ball on the center mat. If his answer is not correct, he uses the manipulatives to solve the problem again and then continues in this same manner.
6. He repeats Steps 3–5 until each card has been placed on a yarn ball.

Center Options
For a fun manipulative option, use small new cat toys instead of the mouse manipulatives.

After each child has completed this leveled learning center, use the skill sheet on page 122 for additional reinforcement.

Playtime!

Subtract.

$$18 - 3$$

$$18 - 4$$

$$18 - 8$$

$$18 - 7$$

$$18 - 15$$

$$18 - 11$$

$$18 - 10$$

$$18 - 9$$

$$18 - 12$$

$$18 - 6$$

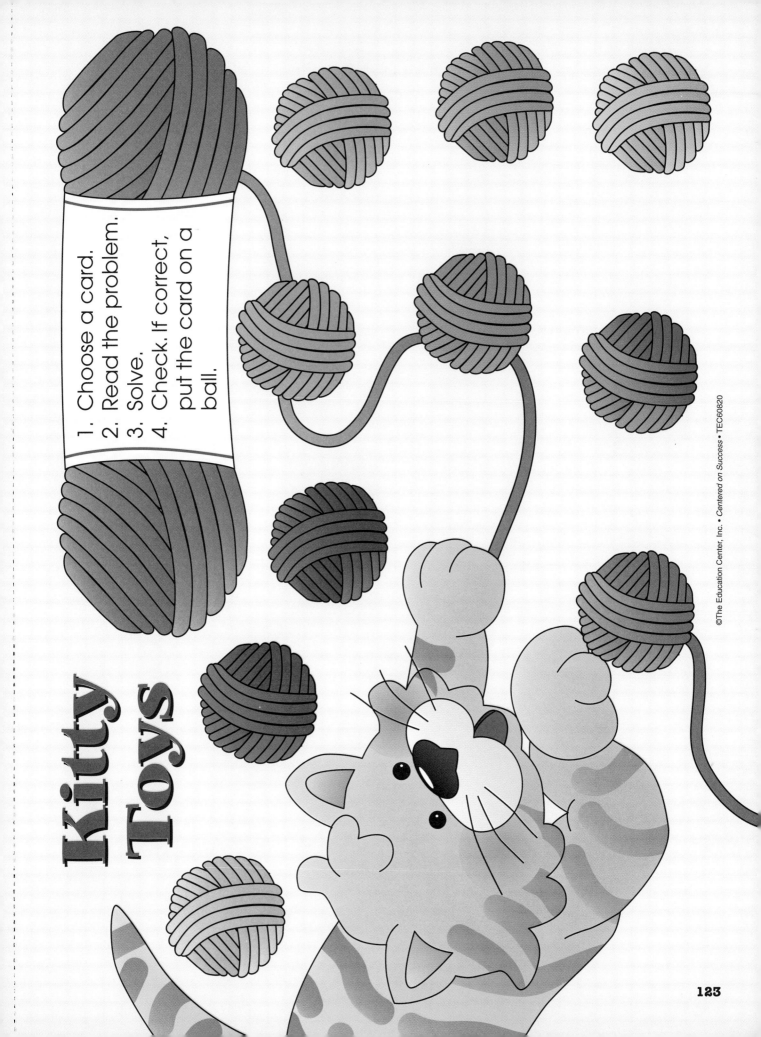

Kitty Toys

1. Choose a card.
2. Read the problem.
3. Solve.
4. Check. If correct, put the card on a ball.

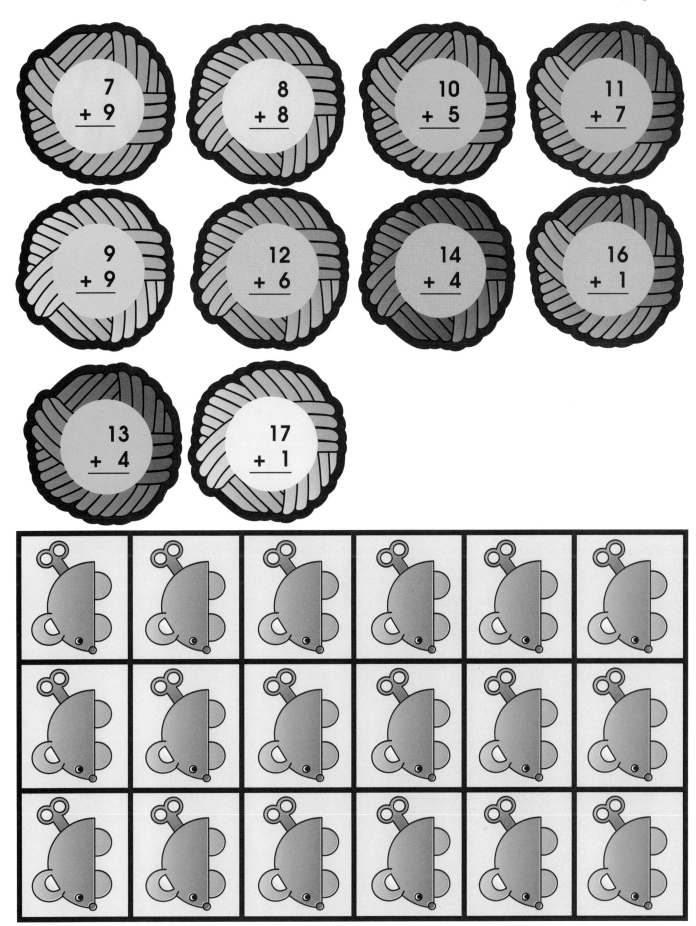

7
+ 9

8
+ 8

10
+ 5

11
+ 7

9
+ 9

12
+ 6

14
+ 4

16
+ 1

13
+ 4

17
+ 1

$$\begin{array}{r} 11 \\ + 7 \\ \hline 18 \end{array}$$

$$\begin{array}{r} 10 \\ + 5 \\ \hline 15 \end{array}$$

$$\begin{array}{r} 8 \\ + 8 \\ \hline 16 \end{array}$$

$$\begin{array}{r} 7 \\ + 9 \\ \hline 16 \end{array}$$

$$\begin{array}{r} 16 \\ + 1 \\ \hline 17 \end{array}$$

$$\begin{array}{r} 14 \\ + 4 \\ \hline 18 \end{array}$$

$$\begin{array}{r} 12 \\ + 6 \\ \hline 18 \end{array}$$

$$\begin{array}{r} 9 \\ + 9 \\ \hline 18 \end{array}$$

$$\begin{array}{r} 17 \\ + 1 \\ \hline 18 \end{array}$$

$$\begin{array}{r} 13 \\ + 4 \\ \hline 17 \end{array}$$

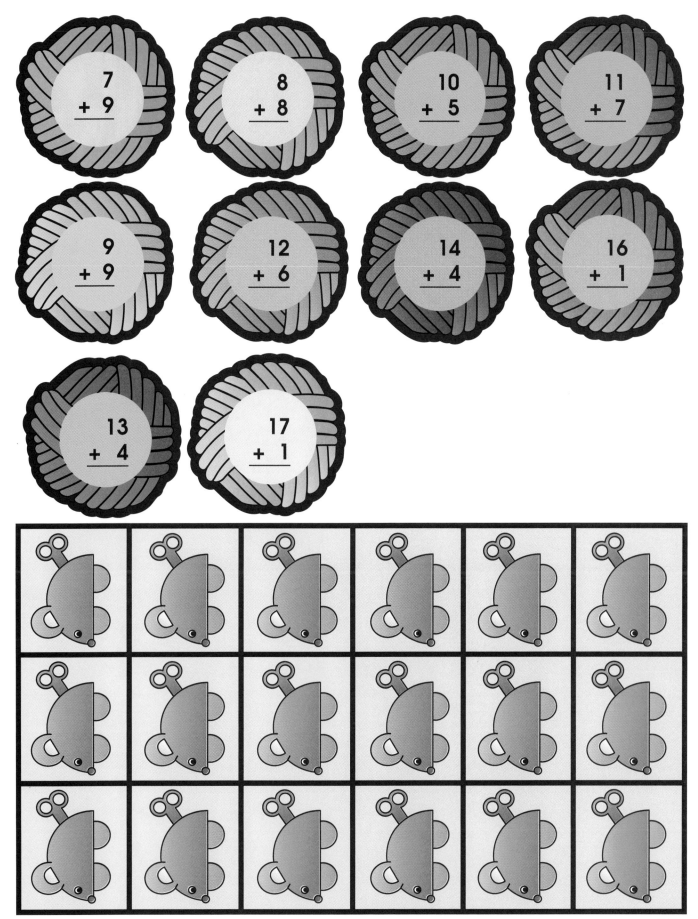

$$\begin{array}{r} 11 \\ +\ 7 \\ \hline 18 \end{array} \qquad \begin{array}{r} 10 \\ +\ 5 \\ \hline 15 \end{array} \qquad \begin{array}{r} 8 \\ +\ 8 \\ \hline 16 \end{array} \qquad \begin{array}{r} 7 \\ +\ 9 \\ \hline 16 \end{array}$$

$$\begin{array}{r} 16 \\ +\ 1 \\ \hline 17 \end{array} \qquad \begin{array}{r} 14 \\ +\ 4 \\ \hline 18 \end{array} \qquad \begin{array}{r} 12 \\ +\ 6 \\ \hline 18 \end{array} \qquad \begin{array}{r} 9 \\ +\ 9 \\ \hline 18 \end{array}$$

$$\begin{array}{r} 17 \\ +\ 1 \\ \hline 18 \end{array} \qquad \begin{array}{r} 13 \\ +\ 4 \\ \hline 17 \end{array}$$

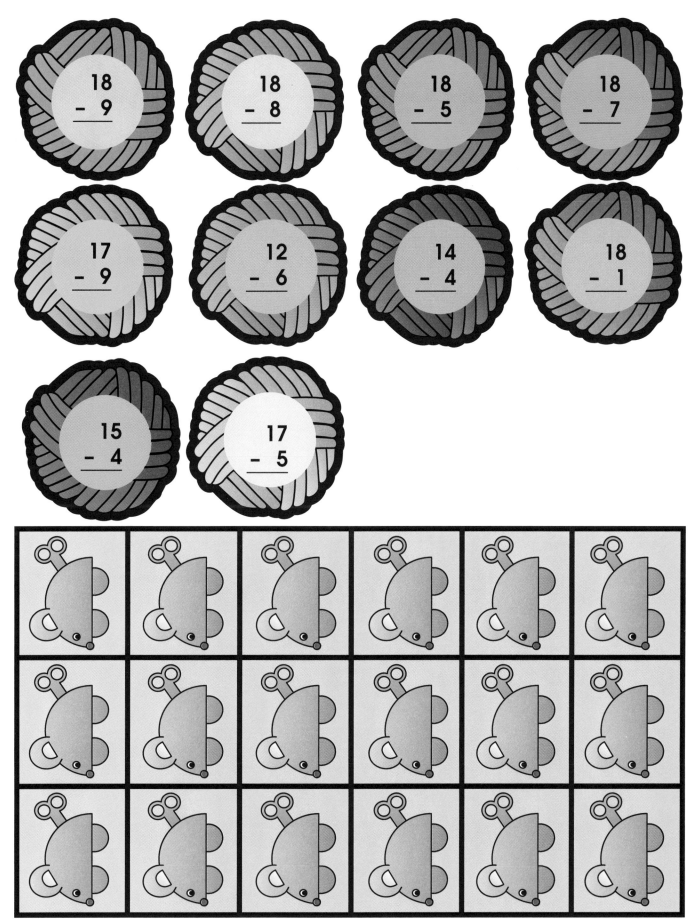

18
- 9

18
- 8

18
- 5

18
- 7

17
- 9

12
- 6

14
- 4

18
- 1

15
- 4

17
- 5

$$\begin{array}{r} 18 \\ -7 \\ \hline 11 \end{array}\qquad \begin{array}{r} 18 \\ -5 \\ \hline 13 \end{array}\qquad \begin{array}{r} 18 \\ -8 \\ \hline 10 \end{array}\qquad \begin{array}{r} 18 \\ -9 \\ \hline 9 \end{array}$$

$$\begin{array}{r} 18 \\ -1 \\ \hline 17 \end{array}\qquad \begin{array}{r} 14 \\ -4 \\ \hline 10 \end{array}\qquad \begin{array}{r} 12 \\ -6 \\ \hline 6 \end{array}\qquad \begin{array}{r} 17 \\ -9 \\ \hline 8 \end{array}$$

$$\begin{array}{r} 17 \\ -5 \\ \hline 12 \end{array}\qquad \begin{array}{r} 15 \\ -4 \\ \hline 11 \end{array}$$

A Crop of Carrots

 Adding and subtracting to 10

 Adding and subtracting to 18

Materials:
- center mat on page 131
- activity cards on page 133
- activity cards on page 135
- 2 resealable plastic bags

Preparing the centers:
1. Laminate the center mat, carrot manipulatives, and cards if desired.
2. Cut the cards apart. Put each set into a separate bag.
3. Place the bags and center mat at a center.

Using the centers:
1. A student removes the cards from the bag.
2. She lays each card faceup in the center area.
3. She chooses a problem card and reads it.
4. She solves the problem, using the carrot manipulatives if needed.
5. She turns the card over to check her answer. If her answer is correct, she places the card in the garden on the center mat. If her answer is incorrect, she uses the manipulatives to add or subtract the numerals again and then continues in this same manner.
6. She repeats Steps 3–5 until each card has been placed in the garden on the center mat.

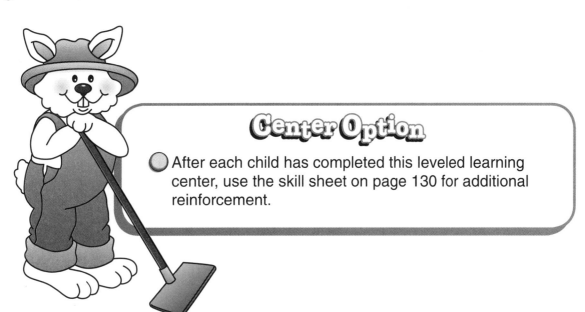

Center Option

After each child has completed this leveled learning center, use the skill sheet on page 130 for additional reinforcement.

Name _____

130

Carrots for Sale!

Add or subtract.

11 +7	18 −13	14 +4	18 −10
10 +8	18 −7	18 −6	12 +6
		18 −4	9 +9

Bonus Box:

Farmer Rabbit sold 4 carrots.
He sold 6 more carrots.
How many carrots did he sell in all?
On the back of this sheet, solve the problem.
Draw a picture to show your answer.

Note to the teacher: Use with "A Crop of Carrots" on page 129.

A Crop of Carrots

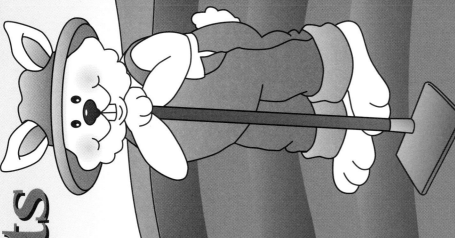

1. Choose a card.
2. Add or subtract.
3. Check. If correct, put the card in the garden.

CARROTS

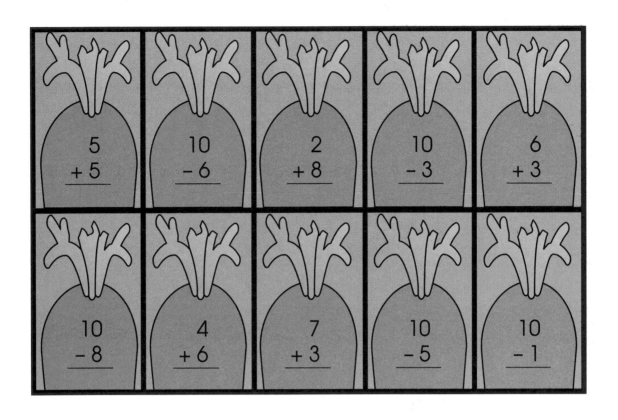

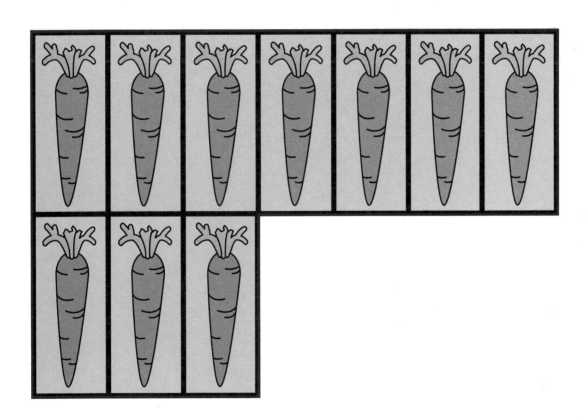

9   7   10   4   10

9   5   10   10   2

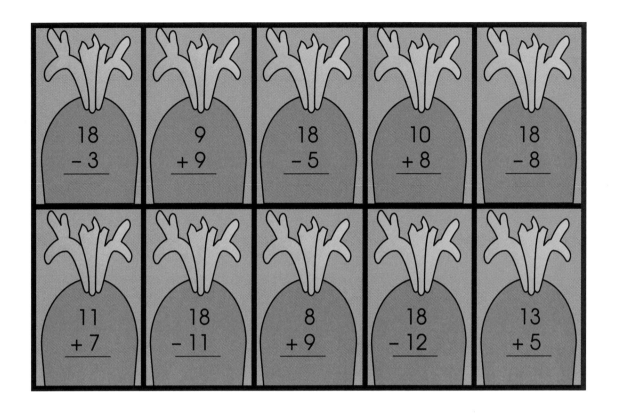

$$18 - 3$$ $$9 + 9$$ $$18 - 5$$ $$10 + 8$$ $$18 - 8$$

$$11 + 7$$ $$18 - 11$$ $$8 + 9$$ $$18 - 12$$ $$13 + 5$$

10   18   13   18   15

18   6   17   7   18

All You Can Eat

Identifying whole numbers and fractions 1, ½, and ¼

Identifying fractions ½, ⅓, and ¼

Materials:

center mat on page 139
activity cards on page 141
activity cards on page 143
2 resealable plastic bags

Preparing the centers:

1. Laminate the center mat and cards if desired.
2. Cut the cards apart. Put each set into a separate bag.
3. Place the bags and center mat at a center.

Using the centers:

1. A student removes the cards from the bag.
2. He places each plate in front of a different diner.
3. He lays each card faceup in the center area.
4. He chooses a card and determines the amount pictured.
5. He turns the card over to check his answer. If his answer is correct, he places the card in front of the correct plate. If his answer is not correct, he returns the card to the center area and chooses another.
6. He repeats Steps 4 and 5 until each card has been matched.

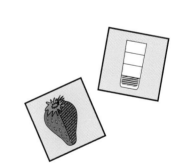

Center Option

After each child has completed this leveled learning center, use the skill sheet on page 138 for additional reinforcement.

137

Breakfast Portions

Look at each shape.

Cut and glue to match.

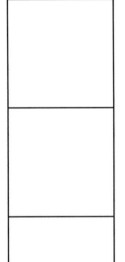  

$\frac{1}{4}$ $\frac{1}{3}$ $\frac{1}{2}$

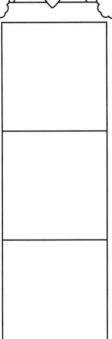

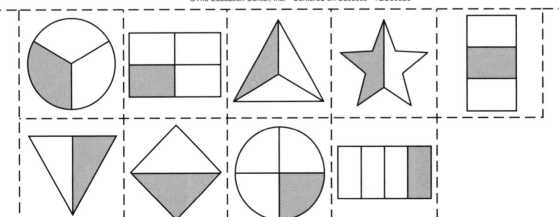

All You Can Eat

1. Choose a card.
2. Tell what part is colored.
3. Check. If correct, put each card beneath the correct plate.

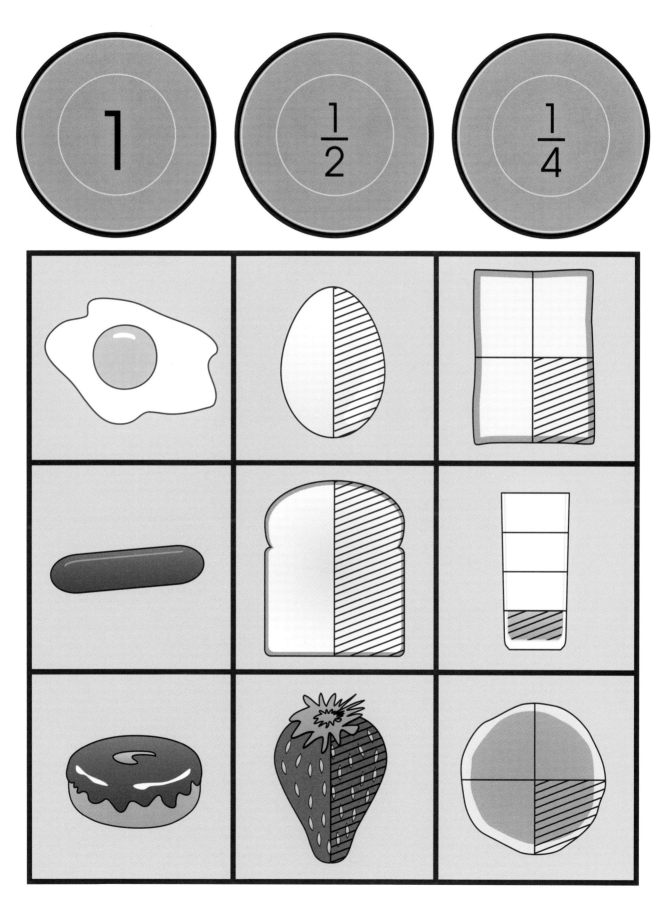

$$\frac{1}{4}$$　　　　$$\frac{1}{2}$$　　　　1

$$\frac{1}{4}$$　　　　$$\frac{1}{2}$$　　　　1

$$\frac{1}{4}$$　　　　$$\frac{1}{2}$$　　　　1

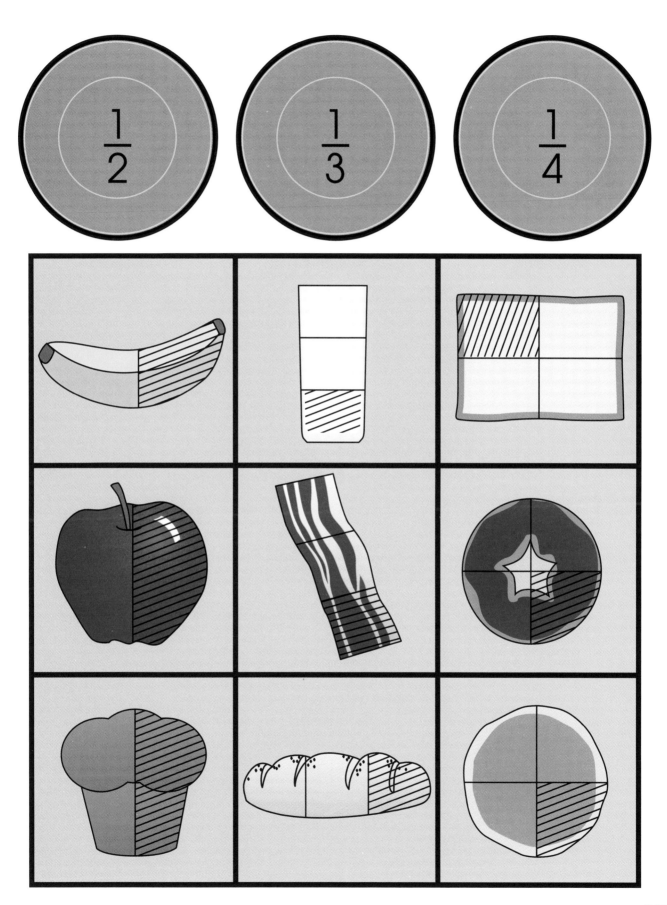

$$\frac{1}{4}$$

$$\frac{1}{3}$$

$$\frac{1}{2}$$

$$\frac{1}{4}$$

$$\frac{1}{3}$$

$$\frac{1}{2}$$

$$\frac{1}{4}$$

$$\frac{1}{3}$$

$$\frac{1}{2}$$

Saving Cents

 Identifying coin values to 50 cents: pennies, nickels, dimes

 Identifying coin values to 50 cents: pennies, nickels, dimes, quarters

Saving Cents

1. Choose a coin card and set it above the bank.
2. Count how much is shown.
3. Put the answer card on the bank.
4. Check. If correct, slide the coin card into the bank.

24¢

45¢   50¢   18¢

Materials:
- center mat on page 147
- activity cards on page 149
- activity cards on page 151
- 2 resealable plastic bags

Preparing the centers:
1. Laminate the center mat and cards.
2. Cut the cards apart. Put each set into a separate bag.
3. Cut an opening where indicated on the center mat.
4. Place the bags and center mat at a center.

Using the centers:
1. A student removes the cards from the bag.
2. She lays each card faceup in the center area.
3. She chooses a coin card and places it above the piggy bank on the center mat. Then she counts the value of the coins pictured.
4. She finds the card with the matching value and places it on the piggy bank.
5. She turns the coin card over to check her answer. If her answer is correct, she slides the coin card into the opening on the center mat and returns the answer card to the pile. If her answer is incorrect, she counts the coin value again and then continues in this same manner.
6. She repeats Steps 3–5 until each coin card has been slid through the opening on the center mat.

Center Option

After each child has completed this leveled learning center, use the skill sheet on page 146 for additional reinforcement.

Money Bags

How much is shown?

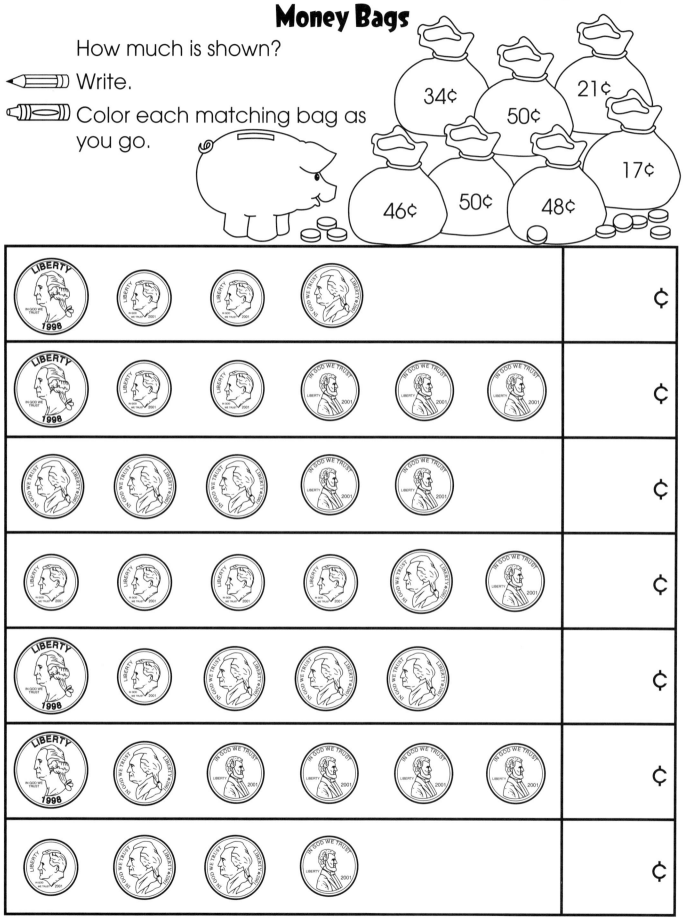

✏️ Write.

🖍️ Color each matching bag as you go.

Coins	
	¢
	¢
	¢
	¢
	¢
	¢
	¢

Bags shown: 34¢ 50¢ 21¢ 46¢ 50¢ 48¢ 17¢

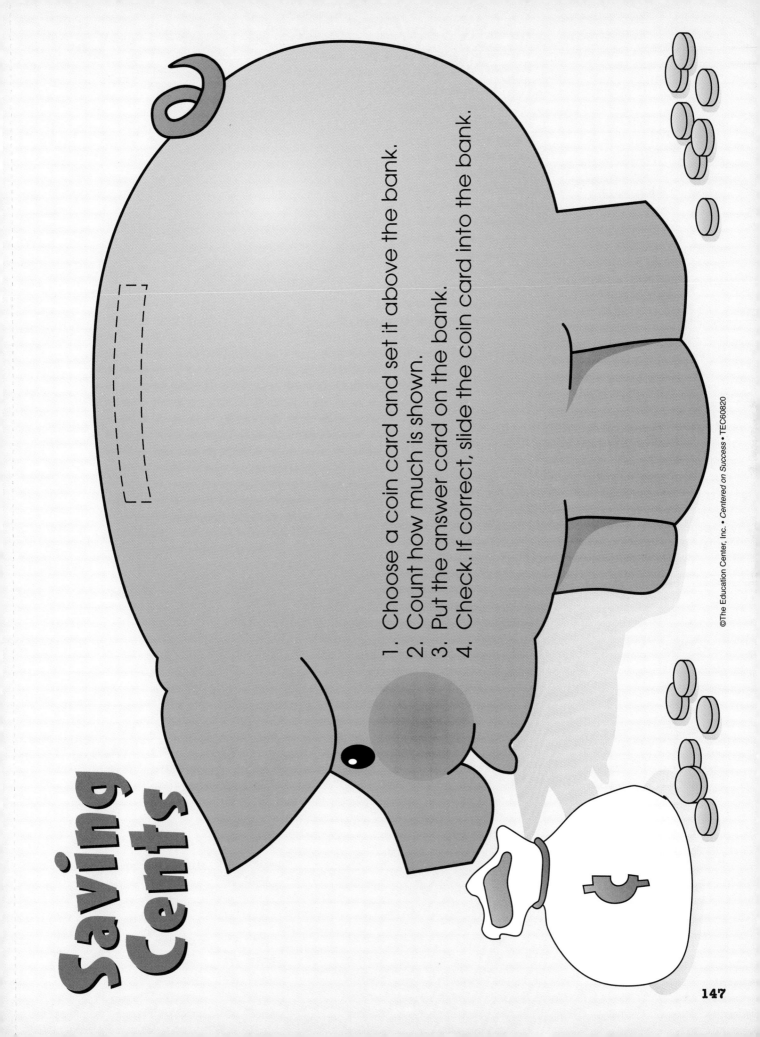

Saving Cents

1. Choose a coin card and set it above the bank.
2. Count how much is shown.
3. Put the answer card on the bank.
4. Check. If correct, slide the coin card into the bank.

48¢	37¢	45¢
50¢	24¢	50¢
18¢	32¢	29¢

48¢	37¢	45¢
50¢	24¢	50¢
18¢	32¢	29¢

42¢	50¢	39¢
27¢	16¢	50¢
28¢	46¢	38¢

42¢	50¢	39¢
27¢	16¢	50¢
28¢	46¢	38¢

Peekaboo Cuckoo

 Telling time to the hour

 Telling time to the hour and half hour

Materials:
- center mat on page 155
- activity cards and clock hands on page 157
- activity cards on page 159
- brad
- 2 resealable plastic bags

Preparing the centers:
1. Laminate the center mat, clock hands, and cards if desired.
2. Cut out the clock hands and attach them to the center mat with a brad as shown.
3. Cut the cards apart. Put each set into a separate bag.
4. Place the bags and center mat at a center.

Using the centers:
1. A student removes the cards from the bag.
2. He places the cards digital side up in the center area.
3. He chooses a card and says the time shown.
4. He moves the clock hands on the center mat to show the time.
5. He turns the card over to check his answer. If his answer is correct, he places the card in the box on the center mat. If his answer is incorrect, he places the card with the remaining unmatched cards.
6. He repeats Steps 3–5 until each card is matched.

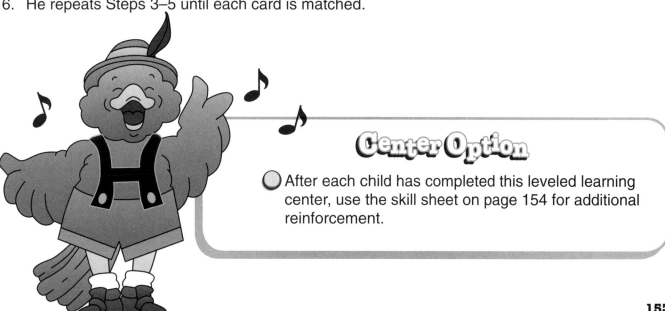

Center Option
After each child has completed this leveled learning center, use the skill sheet on page 154 for additional reinforcement.

Ticktock

✏️ Write each time.

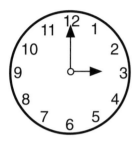

_____:_____

_____:_____

_____:_____

_____:_____

_____:_____

_____:_____

_____:_____

_____:_____

✏️ Draw hands to show each time.

   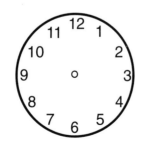      

12:00   3:30   7:00   10:30

Peekaboo Cuckoo

1. Choose a card and say the time.
2. Move the clock hands to show the time.
3. Check. If correct, put the card in the box.

1:00	2:00	3:00
4:00	5:00	6:00
7:00	8:00	9:00
10:00	11:00	12:00

1:30	2:00	3:30
4:30	5:00	6:00
7:30	8:00	9:00
10:30	11:00	12:30

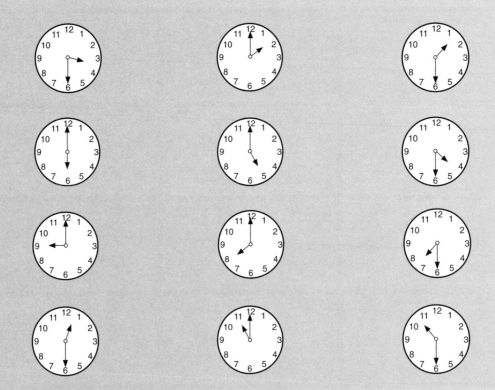

Let's Party!

 Identifying information on a picture graph (fewer objects)

 Identifying information on a picture graph (more objects)

Materials:
center mat on page 163
◯ activity cards on page 165
◯ activity cards on page 167
2 resealable plastic bags

Preparing the centers:
1. Laminate the center mat and cards if desired.
2. Cut the cards apart. Put each set into a separate bag.
3. Place the bags and center mat at a center.

Using the centers:
1. A student removes the cards from the bag.
2. He places the picture cards faceup in the center area.
3. He sorts the cards and places them on the graph.
4. He chooses a problem card and uses the graphed data to answer the question.
5. He turns the card over to check his answer. If his answer is correct, he places the card in the bag. If his answer is incorrect, he places the card with the remaining unanswered cards.
6. He repeats Steps 4–5 until each card is answered correctly.

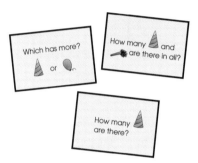

Center Option
◯ After each child has completed this leveled learning center, use the skill sheet on page 162 for additional reinforcement.

Party Treats

 Cut and glue the pictures to the graph.

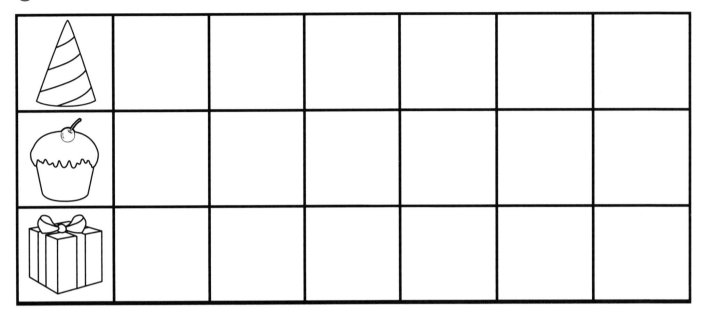

🖍 Color.

Which has more?	Which has fewer?	How many are 🔺?	How many are 🎁?

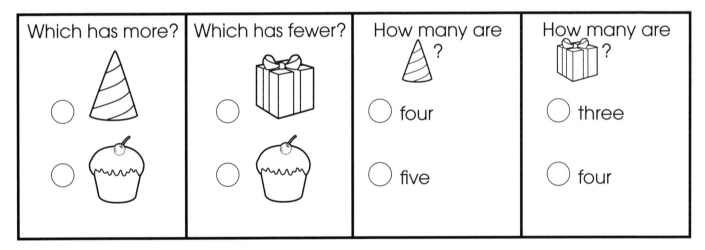

Let's Party!

1. Sort the picture cards and put them on the graph.
2. Read and solve each problem card.
3. Check. If correct, put the cards in the bag.

©The Education Center, Inc. • *Centered on Success* • TEC60820

163

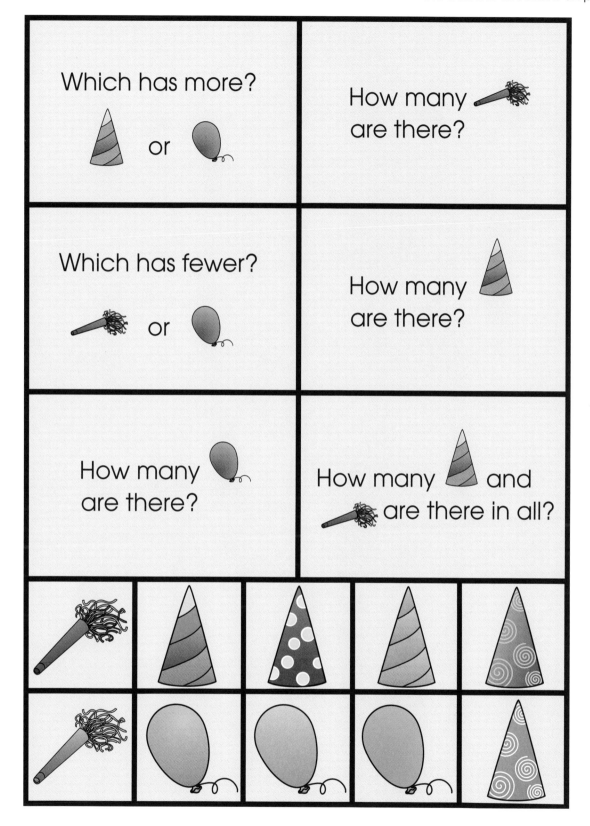

Which has more? or

How many are there?

Which has fewer? or

How many are there?

How many are there?

How many and are there in all?

2

5

7   **3**

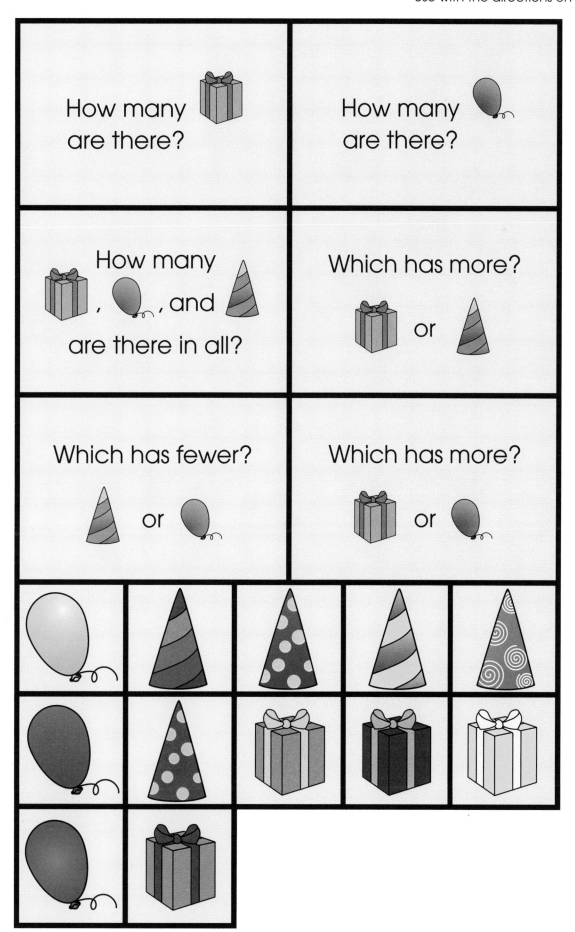

How many 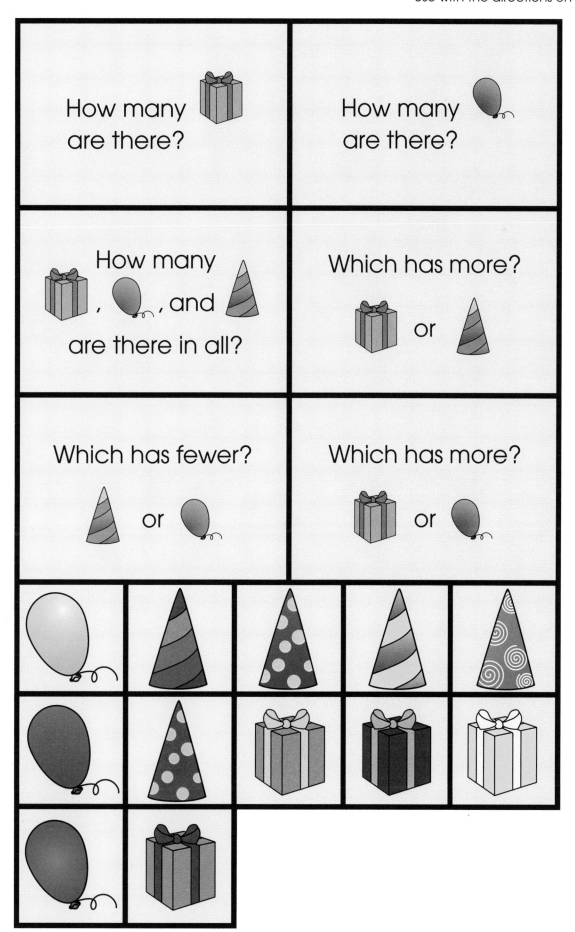 are there?

How many are there?

How many , , and are there in all?

Which has more? or

Which has fewer? or

Which has more? or

3   **4**

                               12